The NPR Curious Listener's Guide to

American Folk Music

D0951282

The NPR Curious Listener's Guide to

American Folk Music

KIP LORNELL

Foreword by Linda Ronstadt

A Grand Central Press Book
A Perigee Book

THE BERKLEY PUBLISHING GROUP
Published by the Penguin Group
Penguin Group (USA) Inc.
375 Hudson Street, New York, New York 10014, USA
Penguin Group (Canada), 10 Alcorn Avenue, Toronto, Ontario M4V 3B2, Canada
(a division of Pearson Penguin Canada Inc.)
Penguin Books Ltd., 80 Strand, London WC2R 0RL, England
Penguin Group Ireland, 25 St. Stephen's Green, Dublin 2, Ireland (a division of Penguin Books Ltd.)
Penguin Group (Australia), 250 Camberwell Road, Camberwell, Victoria 3124, Australia
(a division of Pearson Australia Group Pty. Ltd.)
Penguin Books India Pvt. Ltd., 11 Community Centre, Panchsheel Park, New Delhi—110 017, India
Penguin Group (NZ), Cnr. Airborne and Rosedale Roads, Albany, Auckland 1310, New Zealand
(a division of Pearson New Zealand Ltd.)
Penguin Books (South Africa) (Pty.) Ltd., 24 Sturdee Avenue, Rosebank, Johannesburg 2196, South Africa

Penguin Books Ltd., Registered Offices: 80 Strand, London WC2R 0RL, England

This book is an original publication of The Berkley Publishing Group.

Produced by Grand Central Press
Judy Pray, Executive Editor

NATIONAL PUBLIC RADIO
Barbara A. Vierow
Andy Trudeau
with special thanks to Murray Horowitz

NPR, npr, and National Public Radio are service marks of National Public Radio, Inc.,
and may not be used without the permission of NPR.

Copyright © 2004 by Grand Central Press and National Public Radio, Inc.
Cover design by Jill Bolton
Cover illustration by Dan Baxter
Text design by Tiffany Estreicher

Perigee trade paperback edition: December 2004

Library of Congress Cataloging-in-Publication Data

Lornell, Kip, 1953–
   The NPR curious listener's guide to American folk music / Kip Lornell.
      p. cm.
   Includes bibliographical references
   ISBN 0-399-5303
      1. Folk music—U
   (U.S.) II. Title.

ML3551.L68 2004

2004044791

Printed in the United States of America

10 9 8 7 6 5 4 3 2 1

Contents

Acknowledgments

Although the writing of this book took place over the winter and spring of 2003, its genesis is in the late 1960s when I first became interested in country blues. Since then my interests have expanded to include all of the genres about which I write here, but most especially old-time country music and gospel. These musical interests have carried me through over three decades of fieldwork, documentary projects, graduate school, and now inform many of the students that I teach at The George Washington University.

I could not have arrived at this place without the diligent efforts of so many writers and researchers, some of whom I know personally. The work of Charles K. Wolfe, David Evans, Bruce Bastin, Nolan Porterfield, and Dan Patterson come to mind most immediately. However, all of the writers, filmmakers, and independent record company executives that I cite have helped me learn more about traditional American music.

Finally, I need to express my thanks to the folks who made this book possible. Judy Pray at Grand Central Press patiently and gently kept me on task when I tried in vain to stray. My spouse, Kim Gandy, exercised her usual self-restraint and encouragement whenever I descended to my office in order to work on this manuscript. Similar kudos goes to our children, Cady and Max, who are now old enough to entertain themselves (with proper parental oversight, of course) while I write away. In conclusion, I'd like to thank my parents, B.J. and Wally Lornell, who have always encouraged me to follow my muse.

Kip Lornell

Foreword
by Linda Ronstadt

There's one little rule by which I try to judge all my creative endeavors: You don't have to be original, just authentic. When you have that strand of authenticity in your work, it tends to resonate in a variety of settings—not just the original audience for whom you intended it. People in different countries, from different cultures—even people with no initial interest in your work—start to respond to it when it contains that compelling, undeniably honest expression.

All the music Kip Lornell writes about in this book is authentic, and carries that enormous power to engage people from all different kinds of backgrounds. The music described in *The NPR Curious Listener's Guide to American Folk Music* originated to help us in our work, to support us in whatever our work may be: in our daily bread winning, in our loving, in our community work. And, when we want to relax, it helps with that: with our joy, our celebration, and our spiritual life.

Take, for example, the hard work of reproduction, which, if you're lucky, begins with courtship. So we have courtship songs, and ballads about love—both fulfilled and unrequited. Then, after another kind of labor, the real work begins—so we have lullabies, nursery songs, and children's game songs. And, eventually, the cycle starts all over again.

The work of work, of having a job and earning a living, is often the stuff of folk music. I think of the walking songs from Scotland, used by the community of tweed weavers to pound the cloth. Or North Carolina sea chanteys, to help sailors and fishers keep a rhythm in their work. Traditional music can be a language of cooperation.

Dr. Oliver Sachs, the neurologist, has written about patients afflicted with Parkinson's disease who can't speak, but who can dance. Music goes through a different pathway in your brain and helps you do some things more easily, more deliberately—as we say in Spanish, *con ganas:* with determination, with your best will. We have such hard work in just bringing food to the table, building shelter, fighting off those who want to take it over, finding the strength to rear a family. In every time, in every culture, people have used songs to help them with this work, with clearing, farming, building, walking, getting fish out of the sea, fighting storms, and making good relations with other folks. (If you don't have good community relations, people won't help you shear your sheep or collect your wool. Song is a way of getting everybody to work with one big communal arm.)

I'm grateful to NPR—and to the public radio stations in our country who continue to play folk music—for trying to bring traditional music to a wider audience. The people who broadcast this music, and the more popular, commercial artists who keep in touch with the authentic expressions, are the keepers of the flame. They've brought these songs into contemporary urban life. They remind us that life is more than going from an air-conditioned home to an air-conditioned car to an air-conditioned building to an air-conditioned office. In fact, the only new popular music I like is new stuff that's based on a solid foundation of the old stuff. It's sturdier when it's connected to that basic traditional expression.

After all is said and done, I think this music is somehow in our DNA. The power of it is cumulative. Every generation has added and continues to add something. When you hear it, it resonates across centuries. It's my fond hope that, in the pages of this book, you'll find some things that are new to you, but that you'll soon feel have been old friends all along. And—who knows?—you may add something of yourself to the tradition.

Linda Ronstadt is a versatile singer who has moved effortlessly from style to style, recording songs from such diverse genres as folk, country, rock and roll, American standards, operetta, Mexican mariachi, and Afro Cuban song. Globally, her thirty-six recordings have sold in excess of 50 million copies and yielded a string of gold and platinum records, as well as numerous Grammys and other awards. The Tucson, Arizona, native has recorded most famously as a solo artist with hits such as "When Will I Be Loved," and "Blue Bayou," but also with such acclaimed artists as James Ingram, Dolly Parton, Emmylou Harris, and Aaron Neville.

Introduction

On the last day of February 2003 in Phoenix, Arizona, folk song collector, performer extraordinaire, and member of both the famous Seeger Family and the New Lost City Ramblers, Mike Seeger was being honored at the annual meeting of the Society for American Music. When asked what genres come under the rubric of American folk music, Mike sagely observed that it includes "all the music that fits between the cracks." American folk music indeed casts a wide net. It's a catch-all term for music and musicians who are not in the commercial mainstream or are not precisely popular artists. Most people equate well-known artists as diverse as Pete Seeger; Wilco; Lead Belly; and Peter, Paul, and Mary with folk music. Even Bob Dylan, that iconoclastic and influential figure of late-twentieth-century American popular culture, deserves a place in this canon. But folk music also includes more scores of obscure, though equally important musicians, such as Blind Lemon Jefferson, Lydia Mendoza, Bob Wills, Jean Ritchie, and

Memphis Minnie. This book will touch upon each of these artists and many more.

The NPR Curious Listener's Guide to American Folk Music focuses on the traditional music that developed in the United States between the late eighteenth century and the early twenty-first century. Folk music co-exists alongside popular and elite (composed or classical) music and frequently interacts with its popular neighbor, often informing or reminding popular culture of its roots. Folk music is rarely heard over the radio or seen on television today. Nonetheless thousands of folk music recordings are currently available via full-service online music stores as well as a handful of brick-and-mortar stores that offer consumers CDs and (increasingly) DVDs in categories such as polka, Cajun, bluegrass, zydeco, blues, and other grassroots forms of American music. Folk festivals of every size and description abound throughout the United States. Venerable venues such as Lena's Café and the Philadelphia Folk Festival have drawn loyal patrons for decades. Furthermore, there are hundreds of Web sites devoted to all of the forms of grassroots American music, and these can be found through the use of any of the Web's many search engines. A list of record companies, festivals, venues, and related information can be found in "Resources for Curious Listeners" in the closing section of this book.

The traditional styles of music included in this book are not frozen. Folk music is always evolving; its sensibilities and boundaries are in constant flux. In fact, diversity within established aesthetic boundaries provides an important key to understanding these musical forms. Traditional songs and the instruments that frequently accompany them can be combined in a variety of contexts. The very human, highly emotive sound of a bottleneck or slide guitar can be heard as the predominate "voice" in an African American Pentecostal Church where sacred steel guitars reign over the Sunday morning services, as the heavily amplified lead instrument of a South Side Chicago blues band late on a Friday night, or integrated into the sound of a progressive bluegrass band playing at a Saturday afternoon Elk's Lodge gathering.

Well into the twentieth century, music of all types thrived through face-to-face transmission within small communities. Beginning in the 1920s, however, music began to disseminate more rapidly due to the development of the electronic media, specifically radio and phonograph records. These modes of transmission increased as the twentieth century progressed; today CD players, radio, television, jukeboxes, phonographs, tape players, and the Internet deliver to us music of every description throughout the United States. Scholars have long suggested that the mass media will eventually obliterate today's racial, ethnic, regional, and traditional styles of American music that clearly stem from their eighteenth- and nineteenth-century roots. In other words, they predicted that mass communications would result in the "death" of folk music (and folk culture in general).

It's evident that in the early twenty-first century, those doomsayers are wrong. Although the increasingly shrinking number of major record companies (all of which are now owned by multinational corporations) only encourages the commodification and cross-marketing of pop music, and pop groups and hip-hop artists may sell millions of "units" and rule the airwaves for most Americans, folk and folk-based music continues to affect American culture. The best, most recent example of this is the *Oh, Brother Where Art Thou?* phenomenon. The soundtrack for this film has sold well over one million copies and spawned successful public appearances, most notably the 2002 Down from the Mountain tour, which spotlighted musicians whose work appeared on the film's soundtrack. This tour brought folk-related artists such as Ricky Scaggs, Allison Krause and Union Station, Ralph Stanley, and Patty Loveless to hundreds of thousands eager fans at nearly fifty stops ranging from Seattle, Washington, to Spartanburg, South Carolina. With them came songs as time-less as "In the Jailhouse Now," "I Am a Man of Constant Sor-row," "Canned Heat Blues," and "Lift Him Up, That's All" to an audience for whom this music is largely fresh and new. *The NPR Curious Listener's Guide to American Folk Music* will help you explore these musical grass roots, which will no doubt continue to entertain and intrigue listeners for many future generations.

The NPR Curious Listener's Guide to

American Folk Music

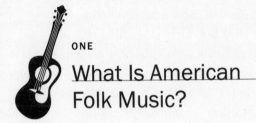

ONE

What Is American Folk Music?

Defining American folk music early in the twenty-first century is not an easy task, certainly not one that can be accomplished briefly and with utter clarity. *The NPR Curious Listener's Guide to American Folk Music* focuses on music with strong regional affiliations or a distinctive racial/ethnic identity as well as direct links with the past. While they may not mean precisely the same thing, this book also uses the terms *grass roots, folk,* and *traditional* interchangeably when discussing American folk music.

In the early twentieth century, the United States was largely rural and the Industrial Revolution was barely under way. Some people associate folk music directly with a time in the past and with isolated, rural (and often undereducated) people. An old-time black songster like Mississippi John Hurt or North Carolina's guitarist extraordinaire Doc Watson generally conform to the view that folk music is old, simple, charming, and performed only on acoustic instruments, which is sometimes true. Others associate folk music with singer-songwriters as diverse as Woody Guthrie, Tom Paxton, Joni Mitchell, Billy Bragg, and Dar Williams. This camp suggests that folk music began in the late 1950s with the "folk revival" fueled by the Kingston Trio's version of "Tom Dooley" that launched the career of Bob Dylan. Much of this music is actually what I like to refer to as *folk-based*, a term used by Dick Weissman, a banjo picker, guitar player, writer, and scholar who uses the term to describe music that is inspired by or directly linked to folk music . . . but isn't.

It might help to think of folk music as it relates to classical and popular music. Folk songs are not highly structured and extended works championed by academic institutions. Colleges and universities, in fact, barely acknowledge the existence of folk music and are just beginning to incorporate it, along with rock and popular musics, in their curriculums. Nor is folk music very often presented in large, formal—often highly subsidized—concerts in the manner of symphony orchestras, opera, or large chamber ensembles. Long, complex, notated works are not what folk music is about.

Folk music tends to be overlooked, or at least misunderstood, but it's often referred to by the tradesmen of popular culture who are forever looking toward their roots for inspiration. This is nicely illustrated by detailing how Keith Richards came to incorporate the opening slide riff into the Rolling Stones' recorded performance of "Honky Tonk Woman." In addition to being a blues fan of the first order, the Stones' guitarist admired multitalented and visionary string instrumentalist Ry Cooder, who worked and recorded with the Stones in the late 1960s. Richards had long wondered how bluesman John Lee Hooker arrived at his unique, percussive, guitar style and the younger Cooder taught the inquisitive British musician how to play with a slide and in open G tuning. So that famous riff in 1969's "Honky Tonk Woman" came to millions of fans across the world from a Detroit-based, Mississippi Delta–born black musician by way of a young white southern Californian who taught it to a British rock star!

As American vernacular music continues to evolve in the twenty-first century, the more often we come up with a "new" trend like artist-run indie record companies, which really began in the 1920s. Folk music forms the roots of American popular music that reflects our diverse heritages, our everyday lives, as well as the ability to synthesis something new. An appreciation for our heritage (a need to look to the past) appears to be increasingly important in our increasingly dynamic, multicultural, fragmented, and complex society.

Despite our ever-changing, volatile, and increasingly corporatized musical and cultural landscape, we have folk music in the United States that is closely related to our family values and regionalism, as well as what we eat and how we speak. These are the aspects of culture that anchor us both to the past and to a particular place in the United States. Highly respected twentieth-century American folk musicians, such as Lydia Mendoza (Tex-Mex), Muddy Waters (blues), Nathan Abshire (Cajun), Bill Monroe (bluegrass), and Roberta Martin (gospel), remained intrinsically tied to the music they inherited. They all reflect a sense of place, which is part of a larger issue, the study of folk culture in general.

Our participation in folk culture is almost subconscious or second nature. These are the customs and traditions that we learn or assimilate from our family, members of the community, and our ethnic or racial group. Folk culture can be expressed in myriad ways—how we celebrate our religious holidays, greet one another, or pronounce certain words. It is unofficial and non-institutional, and we live it in many ways, including what we eat. For example, good pulled-pork barbecue is all but impossible to find in Rangley, Maine, but not difficult to locate in Bossier City, Louisiana. Likewise, finding a turkey waffle sandwich on a menu in an Altoona, Pennsylvania, restaurant is easy but if you ask for the same item at a local eatery in Santa Fe, New Mexico, you would likely be greeted with an utterly blank look! Even sports are affected by American regionalism and tradition. Interest in lacrosse, for instance, remains strongest close to its Native American hearth in upstate New York through the Mid-Atlantic states.

While the United States may be headed toward the time when we all shop at Wal-Mart, digest our news via CNN, and eat at a restaurant owned by a multinational corporation, we are not there yet! Today's postmodern United States is linked by instantaneous communication and interstate highways and is informed by almost universal public education. These factors help make us more alike one another, but we can still discern subtle and not so subtle differences between folks born and raised in Dimebox, Texas, and Young America, Minnesota.

Regional and ethnic variations remain important keys to understanding contemporary American folk music because they still clearly display great variety across the country. For example, the music of a Finnish American polka band based in Superior, Michigan, can be easily distinguished from a bluegrass ensemble whose members live in Rome, Georgia. America's melting pot still steams with a warm and rich brew of Cajun music from Louisiana and southeastern Texas, Mexican American music in Chicago, German American polka music in the upper Midwest, and sacred-harp singing in Georgia and Alabama. Despite the best efforts to market the same pop music stars across the United States, regional variations in traditional American music remain part of our landscape and *The NPR Curious Listener's Guide to American Folk Music* explores and celebrates this rich gumbo.

In some respects, grassroots music in the United States represents a form of alternative culture for many Americans in the early twenty-first century. While we participate in folk culture, we also participate in popular culture. Every time we turn on the television (regardless of the cable channel we choose to watch), go to the grocery store and try to decide between the Kellogg's or the General Mills cereal, or watch the fall fashion reports to see which designer is hot, we are participating in popular culture. All of us do it . . . to some degree.

Despite inevitable participation in popular culture, some folks remain tied to their roots, while others rebel. Rebels look for alternatives in what they consume and how they consume it. It takes all forms: food co-ops, wearing "natural" fabrics, or supporting the Pacifica Radio Network. African Americans, for instance, sometimes turn to Kwanza as an alternative to the majority's commercial Christmas culture. When it comes to music, some folks followed Phish around the country, punk rockers might turn to rockabilly or old-time music, others look to world beat or Reggae. These folks are searching for alternatives to the mass culture that increasingly invades our home via modems or cable television. We are all trying to find a way through the world, and folk culture and folk music appears to offer an alternative to the mass culture that pervades everyday life.

Since the 1960s, in particular, people have constructed a wide range of festivals that celebrate their visions of folk music and culture. Often they emphasize "folk" (handmade, local, acoustic) as an alternative to mass culture. Contemporary folk festivals often symbolize an alternative lifestyle with a folk moniker attached. Whether it's food, clothing, or instruments, the emphasis is on "sharing," "do it yourself," "simple is better," "small is beautiful," "inclusiveness," and "multicultural." These and other allied values are almost always attached to contemporary folk festivals around the country. Folk festivals are found throughout the United States—from the Strawberry Fields concerts that are frequented by northern Californians planning their summer music events to the annual Takoma Park (Maryland) Folk Festival held each September in suburban Washington, D.C. And many of them have been at it for years, even decades. These festivals are largely about community formation and solidarity as well as the desire to set themselves apart from mainstream culture. They are what the early 1960s Newport Folk Festivals and the Woodstock Music Festival (the original edition—not the 1990s follow-ups) have evolved into.

It's significant that the genres not represented at folk festivals or small clubs are either recognized by academic scholars and performers (jazz, opera, orchestral works) or embraced and championed by the denizens of popular culture (rock or rock-based bands, rap or hip-hop). Contemporary folk festivals highlight the musical forms that generally fall outside of the walls of the academy and are not heard over commercial radio stations. Folk festivals (along with the clubs and societies) have become the defacto home for progressive and alternative (a loaded and ambiguous descriptor!) music genres as diverse as blues, "no-depression" country, Cajun, and singer-songwriters.

Folk music is often perceived to be out of the mainstream, which is part of its appeal. Nonetheless, it can still be marketed, packed, sold, and learned in ways that people who are (far) removed from the tradition itself can participate in music making that otherwise would have been out of their reach. The ability to commodify a genre such as blues began with the mass media but it's also been manipulated by the folk forces of the past forty years, many of whom make conscious choices to become part of an often loose-knit and often eclectic community that values or performs folk music.

The popular concept of folk music clearly casts a wide net as well as its informality and the distance that it keeps from the pop music mainstream. In other words, the folk musician is an outsider in search of some recognition (at least among peers), who doesn't sell out, who values creativity, and who won't collide too often with the star-making machinery. This sounds much like 1960s values, which we would have then attributed to a hippy or a counterculture visionary. For many people involved with the folk music scene, most of this will sound familiar, but it will not resonate with everyone who performs, consumes, or studies folk music early in the twenty-first century.

Folk music has influenced the work of American composers such as Aaron Copland; his often performed "Appalachian Spring" provides the best-known example. The influence of "musical Americana" and folk music on Charles Ives (mostly via Ive's bandmaster father) can be heard in his "Fourth Symphony," which quotes from "Turkey in the Straw" and "The Irish Washerwomen," two widely known fiddle tunes, as well as incorporating a ragtime-style piano part in one of its movements. Rock musicians on the order of the Rolling Stones, the Cowboy Junkies, the Allman Brothers Band, R.E.M., and Wilco are proud of their roots and acknowledge them at the drop of a hat. Even punk rockers like Johnny Rotten maintain some of the defiant, snarling, and intense stage posturings of a blues musician like Howlin' Wolf. Aerosmith played many blues-based songs but made a great impact with their cover of Bull Moose Jackson's salacious "Big Ten Inch," which had initially titillated black audiences in the early 1950s. In the early 2000s, blues (and soul) rocker Kenny Wayne Shepard caught the ear of young white audiences. Such musicians are not "folk," but they sound closer to their folk roots because of their appreciation of folk artists Lead Belly, Robert

Johnson, Uncle Dave Macon, Howlin' Wolf, Bob Wills, and Patsy Montana.

Grass roots is one of the key words used to describe the musical genres in this book and it is significant that twentieth-century American musicians as diverse as Aaron Copland and Bob Dylan so often refer to these roots. It's not just musicians who listen to blues, conjunto, zydeco, and bluegrass; everyday folks attend live performances, purchase recordings, and read articles about American folk musicians. At some profound level American folk musics clearly speak to our soul and provide us with inspiration and comfort, perhaps because they are either so familiar or so fascinating. This book makes it clear that what goes around, comes around or (to restate this aphorism slightly differently), what's old becomes new again . . . if you live long enough.

TWO

The Story of American Folk Music

American folk music is complex and cuts across decades as well as issues related to race, industrialization, class, immigration, ethnicity, and education. It's a story that is not easily related in strictly chronological order, however, because the stories of many music genres are included in the story of folk music and need to be related. American grassroots music encompasses traditions that are distinctly African American, European American, Hispanic American, and Native American, among others. Two of the best-known genres associated with American folk music—blues and bluegrass—developed after the close of the Civil War, which is true for nearly all of the genres covered here.

The story of American folk music is largely informed by two significant events. The first is the development of the electronic media (especially radio and phonograph records), which began in earnest in the 1920s. The folk revival that began in the late 1930s and blossomed in the early 1960s (and which parallels the civil rights movement) constitutes the second important event. These events are highlighted by the points at which traditional music and popular culture intersect—the career of Bob Dylan perhaps exemplifies this point the best. Our story, though, starts in the nineteenth century, even before the cataclysmic events of the 1860s.

Formative Decades

American music of all types began to emerge almost as soon as the first Europeans and Africans arrived on our shores. Both the European settlers seeking a new world and their African slaves brought musical traditions with them. They also sometimes brought the instruments themselves along. Europeans, for example, contributed fiddles and pianos to our musical culture. Africans, on the other hand, brought the knowledge of making and performing on banjo-like instruments, as well as a strong drumming tradition, with them. By the early 1800s, these four instruments were incorporated into music making by black and white Americans, though often in very different ways.

Early immigrants also brought with them different concepts about music making. White settlers brought ballads telling stories about unrequited love or war along the Scottish borders that were usually performed by a solitary singer, while transplanted Africans contributed a highly developed concept of call and response that reinforced a sense of community among people torn from their land. Although the races may have remained legally separate, legislating the strict segregation of musical ideas and instruments proved impossible. After decades of interaction, African American singers had composed ballads such as "John Henry" and "Stagolee" and white rural singers from northern Georgia were using the call and response technique in order to teach sacred songs.

As the United States developed in the early nineteenth century, the states east of the Mississippi River formed the core of American culture. Outside of New England and the coast of the Mid-Atlantic states, the push was to gradually move to the west. Scotch, Irish, and German pioneers settled in the mountains and valleys along the Blue Ridge and into the Appalachian Mountains, far from the port cities and slowly growing cities of the Piedmont. In the Southwest, pioneering Spaniards came from the south to become an integral part of the culture of what would later be called Arizona, California, New Mexico, and Texas.

Physical and intellectual isolation of all sorts was the norm for most Americans in the nineteenth century. Most people remained illiterate or obtained the most meager formal education, so that newspapers (often weeks or months old) reached relatively few readers. Travel along the rutted, unpaved roads and trails proved difficult at best and impossible during New England's mud season, the blazing white winter storms of the upper Midwest, and the shimmering desert heat of a July day along the southwestern border. Well into the twentieth century, most of the United States remained a largely rural, insular world populated by neighbors and family that one knew almost always from birth until death. Electricity came to many with "rural electrification" programs of the New Deal 1930s, our interstate highway system began construction in earnest after World War II, and telephones weren't available to the majority of Americans until the 1950s.

Despite the isolation, music making was an important and thriving cultural expression across the United States. Musical activity was, of course, an important means of entertainment at home, community halls, and churches throughout the country. The fact of isolation by itself has ensured that we would be blessed with regional differences in folk music. Not only did we have French-speaking citizens in Louisiana and in northern New England in 1800 (and still do today!) but the physical separation of Maine lumber workers from their counterparts in Oregon, both of which led to unique regional differences. Likewise the long-standing musical traditions of Spanish-speaking Americans living along the Texas-Mexico border strongly contrasts with their contemporaries living in Washington, D.C., many of whom have roots in El Salvador. All of these factors helped forge musical traditions that were built on regional, racial, and ethnic lines.

The traditional musics of white, black, and Hispanic Americans remain a complex, complicated topic involving a variety of vocal and instrumental traditions. The eighteenth- and early-nineteenth-century musical styles largely followed the lead of their counterparts from the British Isles and Spain, in part because of the ongoing domination by England of the eastern United States and the direct influence of Spain on many citizens living in the Southwest. But, slowly and inevitably, musical genres (many of which we now think of as folk) gradually emerged.

West African Contributions

Because no one was seriously studying and writing about these musics as they developed, our knowledge of early folk music is almost entirely derived from a wide variety of primary and secondary printed sources: newspaper and magazine articles, diaries, travel accounts, and fiction. Perhaps fascinated by the slavery's specter and the creative drive displayed by so many African Americans, literate people often wrote of everyday black life. Until the 1820s some writers often noted aspects of African roots such as drumming, singing, and dancing. Most writers, however, seemed more interested in the contemporary black folk music that surrounded them. Visual evidence—especially paintings of blacks performing music—also suggests the widespread development of black American music. Unfortunately, few blacks wrote accounts of their own music until after the Civil War.

Precisely how quickly African vernacular music became integrated into our musical fabric and exactly when African American music emerged remains difficult to ascertain. The legal sanctions against African culture such as dancing, drumming, language, and so on in the New World were in place before the dawn of the eighteenth century, but to measure the degree to which these limits actually affected the culture itself remains unclear. Because of reports of drumming and African religions, it appears that acculturation in the West Indies took much longer. The sheer number of slaves imported to the southern United States indicates that this was true in the South. Except for South Carolina, where for a short period the number of slaves actually exceeded the white population, Africans brought to the South soon learned about European culture and incorporated some of its elements.

Early African American folk music resulted from the synthesis of African music (often by way of the Caribbean Basin, rather than directly from Africa itself) with European music to create a richly unique blend. The majority of the early slaves came to the United States from West Africa, thousands of square miles, ranging from beautiful beaches to large expanses of flat, hot savannah, with complex, rich cultures and musical traditions. Religious and public ceremonies, rites of passage, birth, and other cultural milestones usually contained some musical elements. Because of inherent links between music and everyday life in West African music, it was often difficult to separate music from the events. Most private and public rituals called for music as part of the event, hence much of this music served specific functions from formal court ceremonies to the songs chanted by pole-wielding boatmen to the rituals surrounding death.

Drums of varying sizes and shapes were (and remain to this day) the primary instruments of West Africans and were often played in cooperative ensembles involving two or more drummers, who sometimes used the palm of their hands or sticks to beat out the complex rhythms. Fingertips created yet more complicated rhythms, and drum ensembles played patterns that crossed meter, pitting duple against triple time. Master drummers of the highest skill became highly valuable and visible members of any clan or tribe because they were integral to the rituals. Some of these drummers, in fact, were held in very high status among their peers and were viewed as specialists. Because percussion was so integral to West African musical culture, younger men—this was the domain of males—aspired to achieve higher status through drumming. We can see this legacy today in the United States as funk, hip-hop and go go developed into our popular music with shouts of "give the drummer some" urging them to reach a higher level.

Like their African ancestors, black Americans incorporated music into their everyday experience. This was difficult because of the conditions of slavery, in which slave owners attempted to control all vestiges of culture. Nonetheless, black Americans did maintain customs and rituals utilizing music. They sang and drummed at Virginia funerals as late as the 1820s. Secondary accounts suggest that blacks appropriated the Dutch Pinkster Day celebrations in the Southeast, a day free from work during which banjos, enthusiastic dancing, and spirited and complex drumming lasted for many hours.

The British Are Coming!

Early English-derived folk music is equally difficult to document. Settlers from the British Isles, in particular, brought both instruments and musical ideas with them. Mostly they imported highly transportable instruments, most notably the fiddle (guitars did not become an integral part of our musical culture until the late nineteenth century). Not long after arriving in the New World, however, we began to manufacture familiar instruments such as pianos and to build smaller instruments such as violas. These instruments were used in a wide variety of contexts: country dances, churches, and the parlor of homes.

The Scots-Irish tradition is particularly important in early American folk music. Scots-Irish musicians included two types of songs in their repertoires, which can be roughly divided into dance and non-dance forms. Dance tunes, such as reels or jigs, were played on instruments such as bagpipes and uillean pipes; later many of them were transferred to the fiddle. The banjo, which is so often associated with American folk music, is actually derived from an African instrument and did not come into general use by white musicians until the mid-1800s.

The non-dance forms were songs (sometimes called *airs*) or ballads that were sung in a highly ornamented style. Many of these originally played a storytelling role throughout England, Scotland, and Ireland. While the British ballads include stories about Robin Hood, Northumbrian border ballads, and England's battles with European countries, such tales are not encountered in the United States. The older

European-based ballads that survived into twentieth-century America contain more universal themes with generalized plots: the love of Barbara Allen, tragic events between two sisters, or the roguish charm of Black Jack Davie. The basic appeal of such stories is apparent, especially in eighteenth- and nineteenth-century America when so many people were closer to British culture and lacked the formal education to read and write.

By definition ballads tell a story, but they also contain other characteristics that make them different from other forms of narrative songs. Ballads are impersonal in tone and compress their action to focus on the story's highlights, usually the ones with plenty of drama, romance, and melodrama. They tend to concentrate on the more consequential action (like a battle or death scene), but even the most climactic action is revealed in objective prose. They often unfold as though they were being recounted by a jaded, veteran court reporter who had seen it all dozens of times before.

Lyric songs don't present the same well-developed narrative as do ballads, but they share many of the same themes. Such humorous, sad, or satirical songs often deal with love, work, death, and tragedy. Blues, many commercial country tunes, and most rock 'n' roll songs provide good examples of contemporary lyric songs.

Protestant psalm singing, which was particularly significant in the Appalachian mountains, represents another important European tradition in early America. The earliest technique used to sing psalms, known as lining out, consisted of a leader singing a line of the psalm, which was then repeated by the congregation. This style was congruent with the call and response technique used by many West African singers. Psalm texts were taken from the Bible, while the tunes used, with titles such as "Windsor" or "Lichfield," were not linked to any particular psalm and could be adapted to any text. New England Puritans sang psalms in this fashion and, by the early nineteenth century, their southern brethren followed suite, which in many respects form the basis for the fundamental Christian values that permeate the South to this day.

Sacred Elements

The Second Awakening (1790–1830) emerged as a religious movement that greatly affected American culture and music. This frontier revival phenomenon brought together hundreds or thousands of people into camp meetings, which were gatherings of people that lasted several days (even several weeks) specifically to worship and live in communal, temporary tents. Methodists slowly came to dominate camp meetings, and Methodist hymns were sung in these meetings, which by the early nineteenth century had spread across all of the Mid-Atlantic states into the Deep South.

Unlike most aspects of early-nineteenth-century American life, camp meetings were not entirely segregated by race. Most of the camp meetings consisted of several hundred attendees, but groups upwards of 3,000 camp attendees gathered to sing and hear preaching, with blacks and whites keeping separate quarters on the grounds. Whether standing or seated, blacks attended these meetings, sometimes participating as preachers. Such modest integration resulted in mutual influences and the emergence of spiritual songs that found favor among both black and white singers.

The tunes, too, veered from the familiar European-based melodies toward the banjo and fiddle dance tunes favored in folk music. Ironically, these very tunes were also just beginning to gain greater recognition through their inclusion in

Meeting on the Old Camp Grounds

Camp meeting singing was congregational. Contemporary accounts suggest that blacks often sang louder than whites, possessed more distinctive voices, and often stayed up singing long after their counterparts had retired for the night. These late-night gatherings gave black singers a forum for experimentation not otherwise available to them. Away from the watching eyes of the whites, black singers began to improvise by adding lines from biblical verses and prayers to the well-known Watts hymns, which became solidified by the frequent addition of choruses and refrains. Such repetition both kept the songs simple and made them easier for people to learn quickly. Camp meetings provided the musical background for the spirituals that are so closely associated with black religious music. These partially improvised sacred songs spread as people attended a variety of camp meetings and as the concept of such gatherings eventually spread from the South to other parts of the United States.

the repertoire of minstrel show singers, who themselves were garnered public interest beginning in the late 1830s. These new songs contained enough familiar elements to gain swift and widespread acceptance as spiritual songs.

Although their origins are not entirely clear, spirituals are among the earliest sacred folk songs attributable to black culture. *Spiritual* has been an encompassing term for black American religious folk songs that are sometimes also known as anthems, jubilees, or gospel songs. The term *spiritual* itself was not used in print before the 1860s, but descriptions in travel accounts and diaries of spiritual-like songs featuring syncopated hand clapping and highly rhythmic foot stamping exist as early as the 1820s. Contemporary accounts also list call and response, simple but often times highly ornamented tunes, group participation, and improvised texts as the other notable characteristic of these spirituals. The form of spirituals tended to be similar with an alternating line and refrain that encouraged the textual improvisation that impressed so many eighteenth-century observers.

Spiritual texts are often characterized as sad or even sorrowful. They usually lament the trials and difficulties of a life made even more difficult by slavery. Songs such as "Nobody Knows the Trouble I've Seen" and "Roll Jordan" are two well-known spirituals. The refrain "Motherless children have a hard time when their mother's dead" exemplifies the motifs of loss and separation. Death and escape are two other recurring themes found in spirituals, and it is often suggested that such themes serve a duel purpose. One purpose is to lament earthly hardships and the peace of dying and eternal life, while the other is a code from the black underground. They could also express the hope of "stealing away" from slavery to the freedom of the North. A spiritual such as "Swing Low, Sweet Chariot" contains the theme of movement and freedom:

> *Swing low sweet chariot,*
> *comin' for to carry me home,*
> *swing low sweet chariot,*
> *comin' for to carry me home,*
> *comin' for to carry me home.*

> *I looked over Jordan, and what did I see,*
> *comin' for to carry me home,*
> *a band of angels comin' after me,*
> *comin' for to carry me home.*

In later years, particularly during the civil rights movement that blossomed in the 1950s, spirituals were sung to protest economic and social conditions in the South with refrains about "crossing the River of Jordan" and creating a new vision of America. In this instance, not only were spirituals sung by southern blacks but they were also picked up by the white people (often northerners) who came to work for this cause.

Hispanic Americans

Despite its importance, the effect of the early Spanish American folk music found in the Southwest is often overlooked. Much of what is now called the Southwest (that vast expanse between Texas and California) was initially explored and "claimed" as Spanish territory by the late sixteenth century. This is an extremely dry and warm portion of the United States and consists of several unique cultural and physical regions with their own distinctive characteristics. The Four Corners (the intersection of Arizona, Colorado, New Mexico, and Utah) is rugged, rural, and home to Pueblo and Navajo people. This thinly populated section of the Southwest stands in strong contrast to the urban maze of contemporary Los Angeles, which is home to hundreds of thousands of Mexican Americans.

It is impossible to understand the cultural history of the Southwest without a brief discussion of the role of Catholic missionaries who arrived in the New World from across the entirety of Europe. Missionaries brought not only their own religious convictions but also previously unknown crops, animals, and—most unfortunate—diseases. They also brought their ways of dress, architecture, and music. And many of the missionaries were Franciscans, who held music in high esteem and included vocal and instrumental instruction as part of their objective. In New Mexico, for example, by the time of the Indian rebellion, which lasted from 1680 until almost 1700, they had established some two dozen missions. The Franciscans established themselves later in present-day California, and by the 1820s the order had founded approximately twenty missions, many of them along the coast between San Diego and San Francisco. At these missions the Friars sang Gregorian chants and performed religious drama that included songs, and few of the missions even installed organs. So much of the Hispanic music, especially along the Mexican-U.S. border, is touched by this cross-fertilization of Spanish and European tradition, which began several decades ago yet continues to reverberate today.

Mexico, which shares nearly a thousand miles of the border along Texas, New Mexico, Arizona, and California, has provided the United States with more citizens than any other country in Central or South America. Until the late twentieth century, our southern border was rather casual, with the Rio Grande providing the dividing point along the vast stretches between Texas and Mexico. For so much of its length, one can literally step over or wade through the river—a fact that invites border crossings, increases the commerce between the two countries, and generally enhances the cultural interaction between Mexico and the United States. In many fundamental ways that reflect basic cultural values, the differences between border towns in the United States and their Mexican counterparts—Calexico, California, and Mexicali, Mexico; El Paso, Texas, and Ciudad Juarez, Mexico; and Nogales, Arizona, and Nogales, Mexico—are often difficult to discern.

Relatively little has been written about early Spanish American folk music in the Southwest. Given the historical development and cross-fertilization that has characterized the region for several centuries, the fact that Spanish American and Native American musicians interacted should not be surprising. These musical and cultural exchanges represent a complex series of interactions with roots in the music that accompanies Matachine dances back to sixteenth-century Spain. The Native American population of this region (mostly Pueblo) has been living on the dry and rugged land for tens of thousands of years. When you combine this with the fact that northern New Mexico has perhaps the longest continuously populated Hispanic American region in the United States, which has a strong musical tradition, it is not surprising that this is the region in which the Matachine developed.

Matachines, the fiddle tunes that are used to accompany Matachine dances, provide one of the most interesting forms of Hispanic-Indian musical forms. This style is associated with the Pueblo and Mejicanos (the local term favored by older Hispanic Americans to describe themselves) citizens of northern New Mexico and has been part of the local expressive culture for centuries. The old-style instrumental music is usually provided by a fiddle and guitar duet based on strong roots in melodies found as long ago as the fourteenth century in Spain. In these rural areas, the Pueblo and Mejicanos have lived in close proximity for some 300 years, often in staggering poverty, and the Matachine performances are one result of their cultural blend.

Minstrelsy, Vaudeville, and the Folk

As the United States emerged from the shadow of British domination in the East and South, new hybrids began to emerge as part of the story of the development of American folk music. The seeds of synchretization had been planted,

Pueblo Ceremonial Music

The Matachine is a family and community event, essentially closed to non-Pueblos and most closely allied with New Years Day or Christmas, when we are looking forward to the renewal offered by the new year. Because the Matachine combines music, dance, and ceremony, it is more than simply the music itself. This culturally complex ritual, which includes specific foods, fiddle tunes, and ceremonies of renewal, began in eighteenth-century Mexico as a way to proselytize Indians; today it is mostly associated with either saints or the Christ Child. Even in the face of increasing interaction with non-Pueblos, the mass media, and formal education, the Matachine has survived through more than two centuries of changes. The fact that the Matachine is still part of twenty-first-century Pueblo culture reflects the importance of renewal and faith through the preservation of this ritual. American Indians frequently adopt ceremonies from other sources (mostly other tribes), especially those that are perceived to be powerful or effective.

and the beginnings of distinctly American folk music could be heard in the first few decades of the nineteenth century. The South was also home to most of the slowly maturing black American music genres that would emerge in full force in the twentieth century. It also spawned most of the unique forms of American folk music, such as blues, gospel, Cajun, and hillbilly, that have received the greatest worldwide attention. In many regards the South is the cradle for nearly all modern American folk and popular music. The South is the home of the music that most of us identify as American folk, but it would not have received so much attention if it had not disseminated beyond its own region.

This process began in the 1840s with the development of minstrel shows.

By the 1840s, black folk performance practices were becoming well known enough across the United States to be represented (or reinterpreted) in minstrel shows, one of the earliest distinctly American forms of popular entertainment. Minstrel shows represent the country's first major exploitation and presentation of folk culture to a mainstream audience through its presentation of black music and entertainment on the popular stage. An amalgamation of racial stereotypes and elements of actual black American vernacular culture, the minstrel stage presented a stereotyped vision of southern plantation life—complete with illiterate but hardworking African Americans who toiled in the fields, frolicked to the sounds of banjos, and then shuffled off to church on Sunday to sing spirituals—to audiences throughout the country. Early minstrels rarely featured African American performers, rather they showcased white entertainers sporting blackened faces and playing their own interpretations of African American music. This black-face tradition provided white American performers with a mask of safety, removing them from the daily reality of the life that they portrayed. "Blacking up" became a staple vernacular entertainment, appearing later in medicine shows, the twentieth-century vaudeville stage, even into the era of hip-hop!

Black-face white performers singing and telling stories in Negro dialect first gained prominence shortly after 1800. Within thirty years, popular white performers such as George Washington Dixon, J. W. Sweeney, and Thomas Rice captivated audiences with their interpretations of emerging black culture. Their tunes often followed well-known Irish and Scottish melodies, and the lyrics relied on images of American lore of the black man as a shuffling comic dandy in songs like "Zip Coon" and "Jump Jim Crow." Thomas Rice popularized "Jump Jim Crow" in the late 1820s, taking it to the stages of America and to Europe by the middle 1830s. Some songs that we think of as "folk" and often performed by traditional musicians, such as "Oh, Dem Golden Slippers," were actually composed by professional musicians touring on the minstrel circuit.

New York City is the birthplace of the minstrel show; it also served as its anchor during the classic period from 1840 through 1870. Sometime in the early 1840s, black-face entertainers joined together on the same stage to delight white audiences with their songs and stories about Sambo and other stereotyped black characters. Minstrel shows were actually born when small bands of black-face interpreters added new elements to their acts that helped broaden their appeal. Short skits about southern black culture featuring stock black characters merely reinforced stereotypical views for urban audiences eager to learn more about the curious "Ethiopians" of the south. The Virginia Minstrels, as Bill Whitlock, Frank Pelham, Dan Emmett, and Frank Bower billed themselves in early 1843, became the first group to popularize their format. By 1850, minstrels were seen across the United States and through the beginning of the Civil War white American performers dominated the minstrel stage. Blacks did not become minstrel performers in significant numbers until the decades following Emancipation.

Most northerners, and even some southerners, got their first taste of black folk music through minstrel shows. Minstrel shows also introduced music that ultimately filtered back to become a part of the folk musicians' repertoire; "Turkey in the Straw" and "Buffalo Gals" are two fine examples of fiddle tunes that were introduced by traveling minstrels. Popular songs that have become part of the American consciousness, such as James Bland's "Carry Me Back to Old Virginny," were often originally disseminated by way of minstrels and sheet music publication. Ironically, the unofficial anthem of the South, "Dixie," betrays its minstrel origins.

Traveling medicine shows proved to be another source of steady income for black and white musicians alike. From the 1870s into the era of rock 'n' roll, these shows crisscrossed the United States. They were similar to minstrel shows in some respects, but instead of charging admission, they sold medicine, salves, and tonics. While minstrels portrayed themselves as purveyors of southern black plantation life, medicine shows often played up the Indian theme with their sales of herbal and medicinal products. Medicine shows traveled under names both eye-catching and grandiose: The Great MacIan's Mastodon Medicine Company, The Jack Roach Indian Medicine Show, The Kickapoo Indian Medicine Company, and Dr. Lou Turner's Shaker Medicine Company. Most were operated by a "doctor" who promoted his show as clean, medically sound, and family oriented. The shows themselves abounded with entertainment: theatrical performances, magicians, ventriloquists, contortionists, trapeze artists, black-face comedians, jugglers, and, of course, the pitches of the doctors themselves. Important turn-of-the-twentieth-century American popular singers and entertainers such as Billy Golden and William Hughes worked medicine shows, but the door was also open to black folk musicians with a sense of adventure.

In addition to offering black musicians steady employment, these shows brought various types of music to audiences across the South. Because of traveling shows, rural folks were exposed not only to the familiar minstrel and ragtime songs but also to the ballads and popular songs of the day. You can be certain that the posters announcing the arrival of a traveling

Traveling Tent Shows

Black singers found employment as performers with other types of road shows too. The nineteenth-century traveling troupes that evolved out of minstrelsy eventually used a tent to shelter their performers, providing a more secure temporary home when they appeared in towns too small to sustain a theater. The mobile equivalent of vaudeville, tent shows provided audiences with a variety of forms of entertainment for one modest admission fee. They would come to a small town starved for live entertainment, set up their tent, and stay for a few days in order to accommodate people from the surrounding rural areas who flocked there to hear comic monologues, dramatic plays, and many types of music. Often touring in conjunction with carnivals and circuses, tent shows of the first two decades of the twentieth century featured some of the singers who went on to be the recording blues stars of the 1920s. One show in particular, the F. S. Wolcott Carnival, toured shortly after World War I with a line up of future blues stars: Bessie Smith, Ethel Waters, Butterbeans and Susie, Ida Cox, and Ma Rainey. Within ten years, each of these musicians would be recognized across the nation as stars heard on "race" music recordings.

show and the advance work of the buskers (entertainers who arrived in advance of the show to advertise it) had an easy time drawing a large opening night crowd hungry for sophisticated entertainment.

The very existence of minstrel shows and medicine shows, and their reliance on traditional expressive culture, underscores the fact that the story of American folk music is intertwined with popular culture and music. This process began in the mid-nineteenth century and continues today. But before the flowing of the electronic media (both records and radio), several important folk genres emerged that are now considered quintessential examples of American music.

Black Folk Music after Emancipation

Black Americans may have won their freedom in 1865, but the promises for an end to social, economic, and legal restraints held by Reconstruction proved elusive for most former slaves. Despite the initial gains—a surprising number of blacks were elected to state legislators in the South in the 1870s—this progress was largely illusory. Within thirty years after Emancipation, the highly restrictive Jim Crow laws enacted constraints not unlike those felt by African Americans before the Civil War. Significantly, and not coincidentally, this is when gospel music, blues, ragtime, (and jazz) emerged as distinctive musical genres.

Songsters is a term that implies the performer not only possesses a fine voice but knows many songs in a variety of genres. Many of the black rural singers recorded in the twentieth century were, in fact, songsters. Record companies and field researchers often billed them as "blues singers," however, such versatile musicians as Walter "Furry" Lewis (Memphis), Pink Anderson (South Carolina), Jim Jackson (Memphis), Henry "Rufe" Johnson (South Carolina), Huddie Leadbetter (Louisiana), Mississippi John Hurt (Mississippi), and Mance Lipscomb (Texas) performed blues, work songs, and ballads. Songsters participated in church music, too. After a Saturday night in the juke joint, at least some of the patrons would adjourn to church pews for their Sunday worship service.

Wandering black folk musicians were not an uncommon sight early in the last century. Folk music provided entertainment, and small rural towns always welcomed a good musician with new ideas and a fresh sound. Some were itinerant musicians who, like Texan Henry Thomas, hoboed from town to town. Many other black folk singers found steady employment with traveling minstrel or medicine shows or with a circus. Road shows provided steady employment for peripatetic musicians eager to see the world around them. This tradition harkens back to the antebellum minstrel tradition that first flourished in the 1840s, but by the time of Huddie Leadbetter's adolescence at the opening of the last century, the minstrel show was beginning its inevitable decline and transformation.

The mobility of certain black musicians, the fact that most of these musicians were musically illiterate (in the sense of reading standard Western musical notation), and the orientation of African Americans toward the verbal arts, all helped promote the aural/oral tradition in black folk music. Beginning in the middle 1920s, commercial recordings played a critical role in disseminating musical information. With few exceptions, such as the odd printed broadside or sheet music featuring a folk song, this music had not been transmitted through formal musical channels. Early in the last century black singers learned their music by way of family members, like Lead Belly whose accordion technique came from his uncle, or from older members of an immediate musical community.

Music was especially important for many blacks living in the rural South at the dawn of the twentieth century. It provided a source of entertainment and escape from a daily diet of hard work and poor food. Racism, both legal and social, was regaining strength during the dark decade of the 1890s, restricting the right to vote, reinforcing segregation, and reapplying the stranglehold of economic subjugation and bringing despair to the black community.

Within black communities, public musical performances fulfilled several functions—one was purely entertainment. A performer such as Lead Belly played for many public events within his own community. As a youth he worked at dances, known as "breakdowns" or "smoky jumps" in his section of east Texas. These rowdy dances featured free-flowing liquor, gambling, and mixing of the sexes. These gatherings often served as the social centerpiece for many rural people. From small Texas towns like Leigh to the Mississippi Delta through the Carolinas, Saturday night functions drew the community together to visit, discuss problems, gossip, and relax from six days of demanding work. Because of their activities, Saturday-night-into-Sunday-morning dances attracted adults only.

The actual music heard at such turn-of-the century dances varied according to the region of the country. In North Carolina, for example, the music was often provided by small string bands consisting of a fiddle, banjo, and guitar. Missouri blacks were more likely entertained by a ragtime piano player when they congregated to forget their troubles. In Texas, Lead Belly or one of his contemporaries performed a mixture of lively, duple-meter polkas and two-steps, elegant waltzes, and slower tempo "drags" that gave the dancers a chance to become better acquainted. People called out requests that the musicians could nearly always fulfill, for this was a tightly knit group composed of people who knew each another quite well.

Well into the twentieth century most blacks living in the rural South fit into the patterns associated with a classic folk community: insular and isolated, family oriented, agrarian, cohesive, homogeneous, and slow changing. This era before paved interstate highways, the electronic media, and mass public education helped reinforce traditional culture. The folk roots of twentieth-century blues and gospel music lie in the antecedents (spirituals, country dance tunes, and work songs) that emerged from such communities. These genres largely remained within black communities until they were documented and disseminated by way of phonograph records.

Emergence of the Recording Industry

The development of the record industry along with the emergence of commercial AM radio stations, both of which occurred during the 1920s, really brought American folk music (in its most regional, racial, and idiosyncratic forms) to a more mainstream audience. Indeed the mass media is largely responsible for bringing these southern genres to a wide and eager audience across the United States. And despite the overwhelming importance of blues and gospel music as two important genres of American folk music, the pioneering radio and record industry executives looked to a wide variety of American folk music as they were creating what has become our contemporary star-making machinery.

Commercial record companies began seriously recording regional country, blues, and gospel artists simultaneous to radio's first days in the early to middle 1920s, and they play a particularly important role in documenting the story of American folk music. Despite the fact that cylinder phonograph records had been marketed vernacular music as early as 1890, performers of grassroots American music were largely ignored. A handful of black gospel groups, including the Dinwiddie Colored Quartet and the Old South Quartette (both located near Richmond, Virginia), and the Fisk (University) Jubilee Singers, recorded before World War I. In 1920, the

General Phonograph Company's OKeh label recorded vaudeville singer Mamie Smith performing "Crazy Blues," opening the floodgates for blues and other forms of black secular music to appearance on disc.

After a general recording slump in 1921 and 1922, blues, gospel, and country music finally caught the attention of record company officials. RCA Victor took a chance with Vernon, Texas, fiddler Eck Robertson, who was accompanied by Civil War veteran "Uncle" Henry Gilliland, in the summer of 1922. In June of 1922 this duo traveled northeast to Richmond, Virginia, to attend an Old Confederate Soldier's Reunion. Gilliland and Robertson then took the train up to New York City in an attempt to record for the Victor Company. Gilliland knew a New York City lawyer, Martin W. Littleton, who suggested the two men come to the city. Littleton hosted the Texas fiddlers whose first trip to New York City was highlighted by a tour of the Steinway piano factory. Uncle Henry dressed in his Confederate uniform, while Eck wore a fuchsia satin cowboy shirt and high-top boots when they approached the Victor officials, who were impressed enough to ask them to record the next day. The duo recorded "Arkansas Traveler" and "Turkey in the Straw," with Uncle Henry playing the lead and Eck playing "second fiddle." Eck persuaded the Victor Company to record several more tunes as a soloist and his pre-electric recording of the old dance tune "Sallie Goodin' " is widely acknowledged as the first country music recording.

The commercial country music industry really got started in 1923 with Fiddlin' John Carson, another older musician from Atlanta, Georgia. Carson's record of "The Old Hen Cackled" for the OKeh company sold well (better than the Gilliland and Robertson selections) and a new industry was born. For the next seven years—when the Depression undercut the market—Victor, OKeh, Paramount, Columbia, Brunswick,

Vocalion, Gennett, and Black Patti recorded thousands of blues, country, and gospel performances, which were distributed across the country and sold in furniture stores by the same people who wanted you to purchase a wind-up victrola. Mail order was another important outlet for the fragile 78 rpm recordings; very quickly newspapers and magazines advertised the most recent monthly releases in a series of stylized ads. By late 1925 the record companies distinguished between black and white artists by segregating the series—selections by African American artists were issued as part of the "race" catalog, and white artists were labeled as "old-time," "hill-billy," or "country." Columbia Records, for example, reserved its 14,000 series exclusively for black performers, while secular and sacred country music appeared on its 15,000 "old-time" series.

A & R (artists and repertoire) men located talent and supervised these recording sessions; their aesthetic and commercial sensibilities helped shape the direction of all American music. Ralph Peer, Art Saitherly, and Frank Walker worked with scores of musicians, relying on a network of artists, local furniture dealers, and even newspaper advertisements to find talent. Musicians such as The Carter Family, whose records sold well, came back to the studios on multiple occasions. Thankfully, the haphazard nature of the industry meant that obscure but exceptionally interesting folk music talent like the Roanoke (Virginia) Jug Band, blues singer King Solomon Hill (Louisiana), and the Louisville Sanctified Singers got into the studio at least once. While even the best regarded artists rarely sold 100,000 copies of a record, these regional lightweights were lucky to sell several hundred copies of one of their discs.

The record companies did not entirely overlook the ethnic or "foreign" market. Not surprisingly, the ethnic record market was as highly segmented and idiosyncratic as the communities in which the first- and second-generation Poles, Finns, Swedes, Germans, and Ukrainians lived. As early as the turn of the last century Victor, Edison, and Columbia began recording music to serve our large and diverse "foreign-speaking population" that was already being courted by hundreds of specialty daily or weekly newspapers, which reached millions of people. By the time they marketed race records around 1923, the major companies were already in line with releases aimed at the ethnic market. By 1928 Columbia had begun segregating their specialty series by ethnicity, followed by Victor some four years later. The record companies targeted their record series by country, marketing a series for nearly every country in central Europe. The companies did not forget the rest of our immigrant population, as they also released selections designated to appeal to the Albanian American, Indian American, Bohemian American, and Chinese American audiences.

By the beginning of the Depression, the record companies large and small had documented such important styles of unique American ethnic music as Irish American ballads and klezmer. Although Victor and Columbia dominated the entire record industry, even smaller companies (such as Banner, Brunswick, Cardinal, Gennett, and Pathe) maintained separate ethnic series. Unlike today, the major companies were not above trying to reach niche markets. For example the highly accomplished Finnish singer and fiddler Erik Kivi recorded four selections for Victor in August 1926. These records were issued on their general ethnic series during a period marked by unprecedented growth and interest among companies in American vernacular music. Despite the fact that these two records sold no more than a few hundred copies, Victor still invited Kivi to record three more times (over a three-month period!) in either New York City or Camden, New Jersey, before the Depression put an end to such adventurous recording activities.

The Depression struck the entire country hard, and by 1930 it had altered the record industry's practice of taking a chance on untried talent. Instead the companies relied on proven artists with a formula for selling records, such as blues man Big Bill (Broonzy), country music legends The Carter Family, and Bohemian concertina master Whoopie John Whilfahrt. Just as World War II began pulling record companies out of their prolonged slump two things occurred. First was a shortage of shellac (the material from which 78s were then pressed) and, second, the Petrillo Ban (a contract dispute between the record companies and the American Federation of Musicians Union that lasted from July 1942 through February 1944). These events combined to virtually shut down the entire industry for eighteen months from the fall of 1942 into the spring of 1944.

By war's end a new breed of record entrepreneurs slowly infiltrated the industry, challenging the way the major companies did business. While the big companies looked more toward popular music and displayed less interest in blues, country, and gospel, new labels began taking up the slack. The Chess brothers in Chicago, Bernie Bessman (Apollo) in New York City, and Houston's Don Robey (Duke/Peacock) explored the grass roots of American music, which they released to a popular market on individual 45 or 78 rpm issues. Significantly, Sam Phillips's small Memphis operation helped launch the rock 'n' roll revolution when Elvis Presley walked into his studio in 1954 looking for an opportunity. Within a few years many of the small labels looked to rock and its permutations for their livelihood.

Nonetheless, traditional music continued to sell to a select audience. The folk boom that began in the late 1950s spawned a large number of small labels oriented toward grassroots music and to the sale of long play records instead of singles. Arhoolie Records began in 1960 by emphasizing blues, but today it helps ensure an outlet for contemporary performers of folk and folk-based music. Companies such as Arhoolie, Rounder, and Hightone devote part of their catalog to reissuing vintage performances. Although such companies do not have the financial backing or distribution of the major labels, they do offer opportunities for artists who would otherwise go unrecorded.

The Airwaves

The evolution of the radio and phonograph industries remains linked to the history of modern American folk music. In 1920, some three decades after records debuted, the first commercial radio stations, KDKA in Pittsburgh, Pennsylvania, initiated its regular broadcasts. Within a matter of months, stations erected by entrepreneurs in other major cities began broadcasting, usually to tiny audiences. Within a few years, however, scores of radio stations beamed their virtually unregulated signals throughout the United States.

Early radio stations relied almost exclusively on local talent to entertain their audiences with music, drama, comedy, recitations, and news. Almost as quickly as commercial radio stations sprang up, country music became part of their regularly scheduled daily broadcasts. Weekly barn dance shows, featuring country music, were established by broadcasters eager to serve their rural listeners. Barn dance radio shows were by no means a uniquely southern phenomenon. As soon as it signed on the air in 1925 the powerful 50,000-watt signal of WLS (the Sears-owned World's Largest Store) in Chicago presented "hillbilly" talent to its vast Midwestern audience, followed by WBAP in Fort Worth. Small-town upper-Midwestern radio stations from Yankton, South Dakota, to Rice Lake, Wisconsin, featured daily radio programs spotlighting local talent performing music that ranged from polka to country. The most famous of these shows, *The Grand Ole Opry*, has been a Nashville and country music institution since its 1924 debut.

Radio began very tentatively and during its first decade, this media was so new and so revolutionary that nobody was certain what types of programs would draw listeners' attention. As the Depression settled in, radio stations were found across the entire United States and the medium continued to expand during the 1930s. What began as a big-city phenomenon spread to small cities and towns, which proudly boasted their own radio stations. This meant that even more talent was needed to fill the demand created by the spread of local radio. Traditional music, especially country music and gospel, usually filled part of this void. The centralized radio networks that first developed in the late 1920s brought national talent to local stations. Sometimes local grassroots talent came to the broadcast headquarters to go nationwide.

WDBJ was typical in its use of local hillbilly groups like The McCray Family, N & W Stringband, Blue Ridge Fox Chasers, and Floyd County Ramblers. By the mid-1930s, cowboy music and western swing by groups like the Texas Troubadours (a Roanoke-based group who came up with the moniker at least two years before Ernest Tubb gave his band the same name) became part of its daily schedule. The biggest names on Roanoke country radio, Roy Hall and The Blue Ridge Entertainers (1939–1943) and Flatt and Scruggs (1947), comforted Roanoke Valley listeners with their own blend of humor, local news, string band music, and informal commercials.

The Roanoke Entertainers on CBS Radio

The opportunity to go nationwide occurred to the Roanoke (Virginia) Entertainers, who were recommended to the CBS Network by their hometown station, WDBJ. Their appearance was such a novelty that the *Roanoke Times and World News* sent a reporter along on their February 1931 trip to New York City. He reported:

> It isn't often the diners of the Memphis Special have a real old-time string band to furnish "music with their meals," but that's what happened last week when the Roanoke Entertainers, radio performers from WDBJ, and Hayden Huddleston, the redheaded announcer, left here for New York. . . . They were on their way to the Big Town to play before the Columbia Broadcasting System audition board [and] . . . at 2 o'clock John Mayo, Columbia announcer, introduced the band with "Ladies and Gentlemen, presenting a program of unusual entertainment, the Roanoke Entertainers under the personal direction of Hayden Huddleston. . . ." With that, the Roanoke Entertainers went on the air, playing "Lights in the Valley." . . . The boys played for about an hour, then came sleep—welcome after two wild and hectic days in the Big City. . . . The Roanoke Entertainers, first of the local musicians to play over a national network, are back home today carrying on in their everyday life. For this band is made up of men who work every day; they are not professional musicians. . . . A lot of folks heard about Roanoke, Virginia, Saturday that never heard it mentioned before. Such is the power of radio.

For many country musicians, radio became more than a performance vehicle. The radio broadcasts themselves provided the musicians with meager pay, but they did allow the musicians to announce their live show dates and personal appearances. Thus radio became their most effective source for advertising the true financial basis for their musical careers—lucrative live appearances at which they also sold autographed pictures and songbooks. An immediate, intimate link between the performer and their audience helped these fifteen- to thirty-minute shows develop into more than a musical event. They responded to the musical requests that came by way of the telephone, mail, and telegraph wires; talked about the weather; addressed issues of local interest; and poked fun at one another. Once a country artist worked an area dry and the requests for show dates slowed down, they either moved on to more fertile ground, be it Augusta, Georgia, or Boise, Idaho, or temporarily retired from music as a full-time occupation.

It is more difficult to describe the broadcasting of early folk and folk-based country music outside of the South. The recording industry also largely ignored white country music north of the Mason-Dixon line and the statewide collecting projects were largely initiated by scholarly types in search of ballads: British, American, and occupational. The books they published in the first half of the last century focus on these aspects of the northern white tradition. Comparably few commercial and field recordings of non-southern folk music were made before the advent of easily portable equipment in the 1950s. In the halcyon days before the Depression, the commercial companies themselves did not go out of their way to scout non-southern hillbilly talent. Most of their recordings were done at studios in New York City or Chicago. Victor used its Camden, New Jersey, facilities for recordings and made field trips to a variety of southern cities in search of vernacular music talent. With the exception of several trips to the West Coast and one brief session in Butte, Montana, their vision turned ever southward.

But not all southern-born rural talent heard over the airwaves and produced by the northern-based record companies truly represented local or regional folk talent. Vernon Dalhart (born Marion Try Slaughter on April 6, 1883, in northeastern Texas) received conservatory vocal training in Dallas before moving to New York City early in the twentieth century. Dalhart went on to become one of the era's most prolific recording artists whose talents knew no arbitrary musical boundaries. Some of his records were marketed as "country," many of which appeared on Columbia's Old-Time series. In reality Dalhart's country records foreshadowed the "citybilly" sound heard in the early 1960s. His tinpan alley songs also appealed to the rapidly developing country music clientele who flocked to purchase his versions of tragic, contemporary ballads such as "Wreck of the Old '97" and "The Death of Floyd Collins." Dalhart's blend personified *pop-country*, a term that would not come into currency until the 1970s, and his career in general underscores the interaction between folk and popular culture.

Live broadcasts, often featuring local talent, remained the rule of the day for most radio stations until well after the close of World War II. By the early 1950s, however, the radio industry was undergoing an upheaval, caused partially by television. Established radio stars, including Arthur Godfrey and Art Linkletter, abandoned radio to move into television's more glamorized spotlight. Networks also proliferated, and an even greater demand for national talent caused radio stations to move away from their local identity, resulting in an ever-diminishing number of live slots for regional grassroots and country musicians. For all practical purposes, in-studio musical performances became passé when the nation was engulfed by the rock 'n' roll revolution, and radio around the country began to sound more alike.

Border radio stations, which began in the early 1930s, provided another wonderfully unconventional opportunity for some of America's early country musicians—Slim Rheinhart and Patsy Montana, Asher Sizemore and Little Jimmie, The Pickard Family, Bob Wills, and onetime Texas senator W. Lee O'Daniel and the Hillbilly Boys—to reach a wider audience. Located just inside the Mexican border, these dozen or so unregulated stations blasted their northern neighbors with signals that ranged from 250,000 to 500,000 watts (about ten times more than the limit set by the Federal Radio Commission—later the Federal Communications Commission!). A handful of stations blasted out an unprecedented 1,000,000 totally unregulated watts of sound that regularly reached listeners in southern Canada, though they could be heard as far away as western Europe and the southern tip of South America.

The sage observation that radio waves knew no political boundaries brought Dr. J. R. Brinkley to the northern Mexican border. He had become wealthy enough during his decade of prosperity (pitching, among other items, a cure for impotence using goat glands) to build a 75,000-watt station (XER) in Villa Acuna, Mexico, which opened for business in the fall of 1931. In addition to Dr. Brinkley's own programs, the station featured a potpourri of talent as part of its daily programming: the Bluebird Trio (a female singing group), psychologist-astrologer Mel Ray, the Studio Mexican Orchestra, and Roy Faulkner ("The Singing Cowboy"). Within six months, this eclectic mixture of talent, which was peppered by Brinkley's own "pitches" for all types of medical cures, ointments, and products that were not available through outlets in the United States, was bringing in between 25,000 and 30,000 pieces of mail each week.

The border stations featured not only grassroots American music but also Mexican popular and folk music, including stars such as Lydia Mendoza. Even the famous Carter Family made a move from southwestern Virginia to broadcast over border radio stations from 1938 to 1942, mostly on the *Good Neighbor Get-Together* radio program. They were joined by other prominent folk-based groups—The Pickard Family, for instance—who had also performed at the Grand Ole Opry and had been previously sponsored by Harry O'Neil and the Consolidated Royal Chemical Company. The point is that border radio provided a forum for musicians, many of them American folk artists, to broadcast to a large and widespread audience, hundreds of thousands more than they could have reached through any other means.

Folk Goes Mainstream

The importance of radio and recordings in the story of American folk music underscores the ongoing relationship between folk and popular culture and the mass media. American folk music caught the attention of the emerging electronic media during the 1920s and 1930s, disseminating blues, gospel, hillbilly, and other genres across the United States. The Depression helped stifle these voices; and just as this dark era was beginning to ease, the first of a series of folk revivals, which can be traced to the arrival of Huddie Leadbetter in New York City early in 1935, focused new attention to folk music.

Only five months before his New York City debut, Lead

Belly had been released from the notorious Angola (Louisiana) Penitentiary, where he'd been serving a sentence for aggravated assault. He'd been "discovered" by folklorist Alan Lomax who was scouring southern prisons, recording mostly African American singers and instrumentalists for the Library of Congress. Following his August 1934 release, Huddie reconnected with Lomax, serving as his driver and scout as they visited more prisons that fall. They ended up in New York City at year's end and by the first of the year Huddie's name was all over the local newspaper.

The publicity actually began in Philadelphia, where Lomax and Lead Belly presented a program to the annual meeting of Modern Language Arts (college English professors). Ballads had been of tangential interest to English professors, but this program of southern African American folk songs presented them with new information. Lead Belly also caught the attention of the local media. The *Philadelphia Independent,* one of the country's prominent black newspapers, trumpeted "Two Time Dixie Murderer Sings Way to Freedom." The hype accelerated in New York City with a story in the January 3, 1935, *New York Herald Tribune* that began "Sweet Singer of the Swamplands Here to Do a Few Tunes between Homicides."

Regardless of the accuracy of these stories, the story and music of Lead Belly caught the attention of local community folk and folk-based singers. It was the beginning of Pete Seeger's career; later he asserted that Huddie Leadbetter was the first black folk artist that he knew personally. Lead Belly also influenced and interacted with New York City–based artists as diverse as Woody Guthrie, Brownie McGhee, and Richard Dyer-Bennett. Lead Belly certainly didn't create the folk revival, which blossomed some twenty years later, however, he was one of the key figures at its beginning.

New Folk Creations

At the same time that Huddie Leadbetter was introducing young, interested, and white audiences to black, rural, southern, folk music, Bob Wills was creating a new genre in Texas, which came to be known as western swing. A native of Turkey, Texas, Wills grew up in a fiddlin' family that valued traditional music. But he was also exposed to the blues, swing-jazz, norteno music, and popular songs that came to him not only via personal exposure but on phonograph records and over the airwaves. Wills had eclectic tastes, all of which went into the mix. This music became known as western swing and it's the first widespread and influential genre of American vernacular music largely inspired by folk and folk-based music that was purposefully gathered from and inspired by an eclectic mix gathered via the electronic media. In this regard, western swing is both the immediate progenitor of rock 'n' roll as well as that illusive contemporary genre known as world beat!

Traditional music cast in a more politicized form crept into the American consciousness beginning in the middle 1930s, spurred on by the Depression and left-wing activists who viewed it as the "voice of the people." The veterans of this movement, notably Woody Guthrie, served as role models for the early 1960s folk revival, who in turn influenced musicians like Neil Young and Bruce Springsteen. By the early 1940s, Pete Seeger, The Almanac Singers, Moses Asch, Woody Guthrie, The Weavers, Alan Lomax, and Lead Belly had established themselves as integral parts of the politicized folk song movement. The folk camps (Pineville, Kentucky), craft schools (Penland, North Carolina), and experimental colleges (Black Mountain College) began in the 1930s to explore the possibilities music holds as an agent for social change and to re-examine America's identity.

Politics, Folk Song, and Unions

The 1930s and 1940s marked a period when protest songs decried the social and economic conditions of many Americans. The capitalist system was carefully scrutinized and criticized by singers, many of which belong to or sympathized with the American Communist Party. The struggle for the recognition of unions, especially in the Appalachian coal fields, was one central theme. Several of the New York City–based activists, notably Pete Seeger and Alan Lomax, helped bring recognition for the battles fought by their Kentucky brothers and sisters. During the late 1930s Aunt Molly Jackson, Sarah Ogan, and Jim Garland often sung at union rallies held in the Northeast to raise money for Kentucky union members. They sang the decidedly pro-union "Which Side Are You On?," which opens like an old British broadside:

> Come all of you good workers
> Good news to you I'll tell
> Of how the good old union
> has come in here to dwell

For these protest singers, whose fervor was rekindled during the era of the McCarthy trials and again throughout the Vietnam War, folk music was the people's music, and it served a political end. The period at the beginning of World War II marked a renaissance, a focus on the music and culture that emphasized our underrepresented working class. Folk music came into vogue and could be heard in a variety of informal contexts. These musicians, most of them white and formally educated, performed at informal parties, Communist Party fund-raisers, and pro-union rallies. In New York City, The

Almanac Singers—formed in 1941 and originally consisting of Pete Seeger, Lee Hayes, Millard Lampbell, and John Peter Hawes—stood at the core of this movement. Shortly thereafter Woody Guthrie joined the group, which was dedicated to writing and singing topical "folk" songs favoring the progressive left wing. Their ranks also included black blues singer Josh White, who had moved to the city from South Carolina in 1935 in search of a new audience. For this collective of performers, the terms *worker, folk,* and *people* meant the same thing. They lived together in a communal house in Greenwich Village and everyone contributed to the expenses. The Almanac Singers represent the quintessence of the left-wing urban folksong movement of the late 1930s and early 1940s.

Folk Revivals

A *folk revival* refers to the interest of singers and musicians from outside of a regional, racial, or ethnic group in perpetuating its traditional music. These singers and musicians are frequently young and just beginning their explorations of grassroots music. Their attention, however, can also stimulate a renewed commercial and popular interest, such as the recent attention focused on Woody Guthrie and his musical era by Billy Bragg and Wilco. There have been successive waves of folk revivals in virtually each generation as at least some youngsters discover and reinterpret the past. The revival involving Huddie Leadbetter is often called the "first urban folk revival" because of the role played by New York City, which proved to be its epicenter. During strongest periods of attention (in the late 1950s through the middle 1960s, for example) the population of acoustic guitar pickers and banjo players with ties to traditional music increased. Since the early 1960s, pioneering string bands, Appalachian folk songs, and blues have been the object of this curiosity on the part of the general public.

As the interest of large, corporate entities in authentic American grassroots performers declined, a new generation of singers that included Pattie Page and Tennessee Ernie Ford sometimes moved out of their usual pop music territory during the 1950s to provide record companies with their own versions of traditional material. Groups like The Weavers, which helped propel Pete Seeger's performing career, proved immensely successful in the early 1950s. Between 1950 and 1952, this group sold over 4,000,000 copies of records for Decca, with their interpretations of Lead Belly's "Goodnight Irene," Woody Guthrie's "So Long, It's Been Good to Know You," two African-inspired tunes "Tzena, Tzena" and "Wimoweh," and "Kisses Sweeter Than Wine." The lush orchestrations of noted arranger Gordon Jenkins adorned most of The Weavers' records, a far cry from the music's roots but symptomatic of its blanching. Such an aesthetic compromise appeared to be necessary to make the music palatable to the widest possible audience. For better or for worse, Pete Seeger had become a viable commercial entity, and he found it difficult to negotiate this exceptionally treacherous path.

The Weavers' commercial success had piqued interest in folk and folk-based music, while the McCarthy-inspired House Un-American Activities Committee hearings placed a damper on progressive politics, which was at the heart of the New York City folk scene. These hearings created many unpleasant scenes in the early 1950s as artists, actors, and writers as diverse as Pete Seeger, Lee J. Cobb, and Lillian Hellman were questioned about their alleged subversive activities, most of which centered on the Communist Party. Many lives were disrupted or ruined by blacklisting and some creative

The Impact of the Anthology of American Folk Music

In terms of the folk music scene, one bright light, the *Anthology of American Folk Music,* blazed forth in 1952. Edited by the eccentric and brilliant Harry Smith and released on Folkways, this six-record set was one of the cornerstones of the folk revival that was in full blossom a decade later. Veteran New York City folk interpreter Dave Van Ronk remarked that it was like his bible of folk music, and Roger McGuinn (a founding member of The Byrds) noted that it opened up a whole new world for him. This set was largely responsible for keeping songs such as "White House Blues," (originally recorded by Charlie Poole and his North Carolina Ramblers), "Fishing Blues" (from Henry Thomas's canon), and "Minglewood Blues" (by way of Cannon's Jug Stompers) in the repertoire of singers across the United States. In 1997 the anthology re-emerged in the form of a remastered multicompact disc set (including an interactive compact disc devoted to the eccentric Harry Smith), an expanded booklet, great critical acclaim, and surprising popular appeal. And the National Academy of Recording Arts Science (NARAS) awarded the set three Grammys in 1997, further adding to its mystic and popularity and refocusing attention on grassroots music.

people, folk music scholar Alan Lomax among them, left the country.

The Korean War provided some diversion from this dark period, but the real musical change occurred early in 1956 when Elvis Presley burst into American popular culture, helping dispel some of the gloom with his brazen, timeless message of teenage angst, love, and sensual lust. Elvis and his Sun Record cohorts—Jerry Lee Lewis, Carl Perkins, Johnny

Cash, and Roy Orbison—played rockabilly and pioneered rock 'n' roll. Their raucous and controversial stylings helped move this grassroots-based music further away from its wellspring and into a more commercial and international realm.

By the late 1950s, suburban youth were becoming disillusioned with soulless split-levels, and the spirit of dread caste by Joseph McCarthy and the Cold War. Some wondered if, perhaps, it was time to look back to the more rural roots of their parents and grandparents. As they looked around for alternatives, it slowly became clear that regional folk music had not expired, it merely (all but) disappeared from the commercial marketplace. Contra dances in Vermont never stopped, not all of Montana's cowboy singers had ridden into their final sunset, and the all-day African American "shape-note singing" gatherings in the Deep South had not entirely ceased. Suddenly what had appeared as out-of-date or antiquated was about to become fashionable once again.

The widespread interest in things folk actually began in 1958 when The Kingston Trio recorded "Tom Dooley," a murder ballad that Frank Warner had collected in western North Carolina from banjo player and singer Frank Proffitt. Their version was a million copy seller and its success motivated others to re-examine folk music in a more commercial light. Such trends led to an upswing in folk music gatherings and the development of groups such as The Brothers Four and The Limelighters. By the early 1960s, the revival was in full swing, and the more enterprising people began marketing this music to a mass audience. This was even true on college campuses, as it gradually became fashionable to listen to this music and once again study the printed legacy of James Francis Child and John Lomax's early work with cowboy singers.

Traditional music suddenly found itself back in demand among the general public. Younger people, in particular, exposed to this music for the first time picked up a guitar or banjo and learned their rudiments in order to become folk singers. The music was called "folk" because of its southern background, its roots in traditional forms, the fact that it was largely played on acoustic instruments, and for lack of any other convenient term. To be a folk singer was in vogue and trendy, even sexy. Folk magazines such as *Sing Out!* (founded in 1952), the left-leaning *Broadside* (home to some of Bob Dylan's first poetry and songs), and the more pop-oriented *Hootenany* flourished, with their readership suddenly doubling or tripling.

The civil rights movement and the slowly expanding Vietnam War provided the perfect fodder for *Broadside* readers as well as topical performers such as Mark Spoelstra, Peter La Farge, Buffy Saint-Marie, Bob Dylan, Joan Baez, Phil Ochs, and Tom Paxton. Suddenly, musicians with acoustical instruments and songs with difficult themes attracted record contracts, some with major companies like Columbia, but most with relative upstarts such as Elektra, Folkways, or Vanguard. Though they remained skeptical and wary of the movement's political implications, the large companies wanted a slice of the folk music pie. Their hesitation allowed the smaller, newer companies to move in to fill the demand. By the height of the revival, around 1963, Moses Asch had already issued over a score of records by Pete Seeger, Woody Guthrie, and The New Lost City Ramblers on his Folkways label. His stable also included blues performers like Sonny Terry and country music pioneer Ernest Stoneman as well as several multirecord sets that surveyed American folk music and history in songs.

Indeed, the folk boom affected musical tastes across the United States. Folk clubs (most of them located in cities) presented music in small venues from Boston to Seattle.

The Bard of Washington Square

Dave Van Ronk was attracted to American vernacular music, but early jazz emerged as his first love. For about five or six years, Van Ronk stuck with traditional jazz. A high school drop-out, Van Ronk was determined to make his living through musical performance. He not only played guitar but usually took over the vocal chores because he didn't mind and he could sing loudly. However, by the mid-1950s the traditional jazz revival was out of steam, and he often played one or two gigs a week for union scale and would then have to kick back some of his wages!

Although Van Ronk loved this music, his future as a performer of traditional jazz seemed bleak. Van Ronk, along with others interested in old 78 rpm records from the 1920s and 1930s, used to haunt the Jazz Record Center on New York City's Forty-Seventh Street, where the blues and jazz records were often mixed together. This is where he got a taste for southern blues singers such as Blind Boy Fuller, Blind Lemon Jefferson, and Furry Lewis. He gradually gained a greater taste and appreciation for folk music, especially blues, and decided to make a switch from jazz to folk. After all, he already had both the basic guitar technique and a powerful, gruff voice.

In New York, like-minded performers tended to congregate in Washington Square. This gathering point, not far from New York University at the edge of Greenwich Village, became the weekly meeting and training grounds for folk music. People came to swap songs, look over banjos and guitars, talk about upcoming gigs, and see their friends. The Washington Square scene really began in the mid-1940s, about the time that World War II drew to a close. More famous folkies also made their way to Washington Square during the immediate postwar years. Fiddler Alan Block, Tom Paley (later of The New Lost City Ramblers), Harry Belafonte, progressive banjo wizard Roger Sprung, and Pete Seeger could be heard there on a good day. These Washington Square hootenannies were rather informal affairs, mostly for fun. Van Ronk often performed by himself, but for a while he teamed with Roy Berkeley, and they played as The Traveling Trotskyite Troubadours.

Smaller towns dominated by large college campuses—Ann Arbor and Madison, for example—supported folk music venues. Nonetheless, New York remained at the commercial and artistic vortex of this revival movement. In New York City, Asch also gave voice to newer and younger folk-based singers like singer-guitarist Dave Van Ronk, who resided at the center of the revival and continued performing until his death late in 2002.

Singer-Songwriters

The folk scene became more serious, too, as people decided to try to make a living from playing folk music. The Folk Singers Guild was one response to this new interest in traditional music. Though not an all-encompassing organization, the Folk Singers Guild nonetheless affected the New York City folk scene. The hundred or so members were mostly, but not all, musicians. Washington Square near Greenwich Village, served as the primary venue for most guild members; however, it also organized a few small concerts in local halls, such as Gerdes Folk City, which opened in 1961, and Izzy Young's Folklore Center on McDougal Street.

Traditional music first caught the attention of Judy Collins and Bob Dylan, but after several years they moved on to perform more original material. When they began writing their own songs, their albums and live performances mixed folk songs with these self-penned verses. Slowly these muscians moved into the popular mainstream by adding electric instruments and even lush string orchestrations.

This process was repeated many times, spawning the singer-songwriter movement that touched American popular music in the middle to late 1960s. Once again we see the symbiotic interchange among corporate America, popular culture, and our own grassroots. Professional performers, including Buffy St. Marie, Pete Seeger, Tom Paxton, and Joan Baez, inarguably helped ignite a minor musical revolution based on the earlier blues, gospel, and country artists they so admired. However their careers also intertwined with the cultural upheaval of the 1960s, and they soon moved exclusively into folk-based music and eventually more popular styles.

Most of the commercial and popular interest in singer-songwriters focused on younger, city-bred performers, and Bob Dylan emerged as the one performer who the major companies could not ignore. After shifting his home from Hibbing, Minnesota, to New York City in 1959, Dylan's personality and music gradually affected this burgeoning scene. *Broadside* magazine published his songs "Masters of War," "Blowin' in the Wind," and "It's All Right," and he appeared on the cover of *Sing Out!* in October 1962. Dylan himself was dismissed as a performer early in his career. "Can't sing, can't play . . . nothing special" was the rap against him. However he not only caught the attention of commercial folk-based music enthusiasts but also the ear of Columbia Record executive John Hammond who had previously committed Count Basie and Billie Holiday (and, later, Bruce Springsteen) to contracts. In late 1963, Bob Dylan became a Columbia Record artist.

Bob Dylan has profoundly affected American popular music and culture. Except for his early recording (on harmonica) with Mississippi blues man Big Joe Williams, Dylan's music had few direct connections with regional or racial genres of American folk music. He was genuinely inspired by Woody Guthrie, Pete Seeger, and others and continues to acknowledge his debt to the genre. The blues also struck Dylan as powerful music, but his most significant contribution lies with topical songs and more personal messages aimed at a general audience. Dylan provides the quintessential example of folk-based music reaching a mainstream, popular audience. The importance of this distinction becomes clearer in light of Dylan's audiences beginning in 1963 and escalating two years later, after his fabled Newport Folk Festival appearance.

The famous August 28, 1963, March on Washington, during which Martin Luther King Jr. delivered his renowned "I Have a Dream" speech was attended by Joan Baez, Bob Dylan, and many other city-billy commercial folk singers. Dylan lent his heartfelt support to the voting rights and civil rights movement in an event that drew international attention. And he was not the only one to sing out about social injustice and problems. Their course had been charted many years before by The Almanac Singers, The Weavers, and others. Tom Paxton, Peter Krug, Phil Ochs, and countless others felt it their duty to comment on topical issues of the day, but they also wrote songs based on their own personal discontent, malaise, and social injustice. This trait set them apart from their earlier models and established clear precedents for the careers of popular singer-songwriters such as Joni Mitchell, Tom Rush, Cat Stevens, and Neil Young. These folks, in turn, influenced younger European-born pop performers like Sting and Bono, both of whom have demonstrated a social conscious in their songwriting while reaching massive audiences.

Newport, Bob Dylan, and Folk-Rock

Although television shows like ABC's *Hootenanny* were broadcast to audiences nationwide, the apex of the folk revival came with the 1963 Newport Folk Festival. This gathering of protest singers, topical songwriters, commercial folk groups, and traditional musicians—such as Doc Watson, Frank Proffitt, and Clarence Ashley—drew an unprecedented huge crowd of 37,000 people and made a major media splash. Music festivals were nothing new; fiddle contests had been held in the South for decades, and Newport itself had been home to jazz festivals since the 1950s. But the 1963 Newport Folk Festival stood as the largest such conclave and a raving success, deemed as such from both the popular press and within the folk community. Its $70,000 profit also underscored the commercial viability of this music.

But the year 1965 marked *the* dramatic change in commercial folk music. After a halcyon half a decade of success, commercial exposure, and a wave of recordings, Bob Dylan's appearance at the Newport festival rocked the relatively small world of American folk music. Dylan possessed a public persona that had begun to conflict with the event's self-perception. His motorcycle jacket and electric guitar brought Dylan immediate disfavor. He violated a well-established perception that folk music can't be played on anything that needs to be plugged in—never mind that many country blues players had been using electric guitars for more than a decade. His appearance caused a near riot and marked a shift toward a hybrid that was dubbed folk-rock.

Dylan had transcended his role as a folksinger but was not entirely clear about being an American spokesperson. The moralizing tone of his early songs was tempered by uncertainty and the feeling that he might not have all of the answers. His new persona, so quickly and unexpectedly revealed at Newport, had serious repercussions within the community of commercial folk singers. Over cups of coffee and in the folk press, the debate raged over this turn of events: Had Dylan sold out, where was folk music headed, had the focus been lost, was folk music becoming too commercial?

Folk-Rockin' and the Blues

The folk revival was not confined to New York City and New England. Coffee houses and small clubs offered folk entertainment in cities and college campuses across the country. A few musicians caught up in this movement branched out in a new direction too. Erik Darling, Roger Sprung, Bela Fleck, and Billy Faier all began their careers by learning to play old-time or bluegrass. But within a few years, they began bringing elements of jazz and influences from non-Western music into their playing. These experimenters from the 1960s, whose ranks included Jerry Garcia whose early gigs with a Bay Area jug band and several bluegrass bands eventually morphed into the Grateful Dead, found only a small audience for their hybrids and were about forty years ahead of their time. By the early 2000s, these bands seemed to be much closer to the mainstream, in the form of "jam bands," such as Phish.

From a purely commercial perspective, the folk revival (albeit diminished) lasted into the late 1960s, creating hybrids, such as the folk-rock of The Byrds and The Flying Burrito Brothers, who reached across the United States with their blend brewed at clubs like the Ash Grove in Los Angeles. Post-1965 Dylan can also be considered a folk-rocker. His records with The Band are particularly fine examples of folk-based rock music. The careers of Simon and Garfunkle, Tim Hardin, and Leonard Cohen also benefited from this movement. On the

West Coast, folk-rock was smoothed out yet more and popularized by The Mamas and the Papas as well as by Sonny and Cher. The peak of commercial success for folk-inspired rock and pop music was 1965 and 1966.

Significantly, most of the British groups that rose to prominence in the mid-1960s displayed a strong propensity toward American vernacular culture and music. Led by The Beatles, The Rolling Stones, and The Who, British groups assaulted our popular culture with their unique hybrid of electric guitars, working-class English sensibilities, and a distinctive love for black American music. Many of these musicians had been attracted to this music during the skiffle-band (a British version of folk music mixed with rockabilly) era of the middle to late 1950s. This led many British youth to discover the imported recordings of Howlin' Wolf, Chuck Berry, Robert Johnson, Muddy Waters, Memphis Minnie, and Lead Belly. The middle 1960s saw cover versions of American blues music by English rock groups, who appeared on radios and records in homes across the United States. American youth raved over The Rolling Stones' version of Howling Wolf's "Little Red Rooster," Cream's cover of "Outside Woman Blues" (originally by Blind Willie Reynolds), Sonny Boy Williamson's "Eyesight to the Blind" by The Who, and Led Zeppelin's rendition of "You Shook Me" (penned by Willie Dixon). No doubt only the most hip American listeners understood the arcane British allusions to blues culture, such as the fact that The Moody Blues are named for a song performed by Louisiana harp blower Slim Harpo in 1963.

This lionization of the African American blues tradition by European rock stars led not only to increased record sales and tours overseas but also to a renewed interest in the United States, most significantly among young whites. Worn copies of race records began appearing on tapes that circulated within a small circle of dedicated fans, and in 1964 Origin Jazz Library (OJL) became the first record company devoted to reissuing this music on long-playing records. The interest on the part of younger whites also resulted in the rediscovery of older blues musicians who had recorded in the 1920s and 1930s. Using clues gleaned from race records, Tom Hoskins, Nick Perls, John Fahey, and others traveled across the Deep South to find Robert Wilkins, Skip James, Eddie "Son" House, Mississippi John Hurt, and Bukka White. These men launched new, albeit brief, musical careers complete with concert tours and recordings. Due to declining health or shifts in interests, other surviving musicians from this era— Gus Cannon, Memphis Minnie, Peg-Leg Howell, or Kokomo Arnold, for example—only marginally benefited from the revival.

Even the movement to locate black blues singers was not unique to the mid-1960s. Alan Lomax was scouring northern Mississippi for the late Robert Johnson when he located Muddy Waters on Stovall's Plantation in 1941. Samuel Charters traveled to Memphis as early as 1954 to speak with Furry Lewis, Will Shade, Milton Robie, and other veterans. The primary differences were the development of a younger (nearly entirely white) audience for blues, making concert tours and the sales of albums possible. Their way was paved by the folk revival of the early 1960s, followed by the blues boom a few years later.

These shifts also underscore important changes in the consumption of this vital form of American folk music. The blues boom existed through the support of white audiences, not under the aegis of black listeners. Folk blues singers in the 1960s often played in coffee houses and concert halls, although in the rural South, musicians such as R. L. Burnside continued to labor in the juke joints and rough clubs of northeastern

Mississippi. While the blues revival affirmed that not all of the older blues singers had died with the advent of rock 'n' roll and soul music, it also reaffirmed that this tenacious music still enjoyed some grassroots support. Not only was Burnside still playing blues but other "unknowns" such as Baby Tate, Mance Lipscomb, Bill Williams, Elizabeth Cotton, Elester Anderson, and Jack Owens had kept the tradition going. Today, however, this grassroots support from the black community is all but gone—the blues has been commodified to such a degree that its base of support is virtually all white.

New Voices, New Venues

The renewed interest in American folk music inevitably resulted in a new generation of interpreters whose backgrounds were usually antithetical to the roots and upbringing of the musicians whom they idolized. Many of the revivalists were younger northern musicians attracted to the wide variety of roots music they heard on Folkways or Vanguard Records or saw at folk festivals from Berkeley to Philadelphia. Unlike groups such as The Limelighters or The Kingston Trio, most of these musicians tended to learn this music directly from the masters and faithfully reproduce it. They viewed themselves as carriers of the torch passed from one generation to the other, often fearing that younger members of the community had ignored this music in favor of more contemporary forms: bluegrass, soul, Nashville country, or R&B.

This trend resulted in new performance venues and avenues for both traditional musicians and those who have revived and interpreted earlier styles. A circuit of festivals, coffee houses, and small concert halls catering to folk music devotees developed across the country. This circuit supported musical programs by a variety of artists, ranging from a semiretired blues

Returning to the Mountains

Not surprisingly, parallel activity was occurring in white folk music as younger scholars and collectors rediscovered their roots. The talented multi-instrumentalist Mike Seeger of the Seeger family, which included Pete, Charles (an eminent musicologist), Ruth (a composer), Peggy (another musician), and Tony (an ethnomusicologist), became seriously interested in bluegrass and old-time music in the middle 1950s. By the late 1950s, he and two other city-billy musicians, John Cohen and Tom Paley, formed The New Lost City Ramblers, the first of the truly conscious revival string bands to explore the many avenues of their roots. The New Lost City Ramblers performed many types of American folk music, though most of it emanated from the South. Many younger people were first exposed to string-band music through the ensemble work of the Ramblers. They learned their music directly from folk musicians, older records, and field recordings.

Not only did these people rediscover the first generation of recording artists but these new collectors found a thriving group of musicians who had never left the South and who had not been preserved on records. Important "new" traditional singers such as Roscoe Holcomb in eastern Kentucky and ballad singer Dillard Chandler, who lived near Asheville, North Carolina, made field recordings that were eventually released on Folkways. Cohen also introduced a new medium to the folk revival—the ethnographic documentary film that resulted in short films devoted to Holcomb and Chandler. He has continued to produce films, and his most important statement on the subject is *Musical Holdouts,* which addressed regional genres of American music.

performer Sleepy John Estes, to an ensemble that revived the contra-dance music they heard at a town hall in southern New Hampshire, or a string band that learned at the feet of Wade Ward in Galax, Virginia.

In the early 1970s, Rounder Records emerged at the vanguard of recording and disseminating American grassroots music. Rounder began as an "anti-profit collective" but thirty years later it's become a minor conglomerate, having assimilated Flying Fish and several other small labels. The hundreds of issues of old-time, bluegrass, blues, Cajun, and other forms of grassroots and ethnic music is the largest in the United States and appears on such subsidiary labels as Bullseye Blues. They have also lead the way in reissuing important material overlooked by major companies, such releasing the complete (RCA Victor) works of The Carter Family and Jimmie Rodgers on compact discs as well as a 6-CD sampler of Huddie Leadbetter's recordings for the Library of Congress. And, of course, Rounder is carefully revisiting the career of Alan Lomax with the release of approximately 120 CDs of his material over a ten-year period!

Hundreds of thousands of music fans have been exposed to a wide range of music by these means and to performers with increasingly eclectic repertoires. It's now possible to hear groups with tongue-in-cheek names such as The Mighty Possums, Mice in the Attic, and Moose Chowder. Many of these bands unblinkingly mix Irish tunes, western swing, British ballads, rockabilly, and southern fiddle tunes. Revival bands of all descriptions have become the staple ensemble for many young white instrumentalists interested in alternatives to popular music groups.

The folk music revival has also renewed interest in ethnic traditions. Ethnic traditions have always existed in their communities—like blues and hillbilly music they never "died."

Unlike these two genres, other traditional ethnic musics have never really moved beyond their grassroots audiences to become part of popular culture. This is partly the result of language differences—songs with the words sung in Yiddish, Swedish, Ukrainian, or Spanish are unintelligible to those whose tongue is English.

The ghettoization of ethnic music is also related to the relative inaccessibility of mass media, particularly radio and record companies. Except for those serving a major urban center or smaller community dominated by members of a certain cultural or language group, most radio stations do not serve the musical needs of ethnic groups. Similarly, record companies generally do not sell enough discs to warrant paying much attention to foreign-language records. In this case, there simply is not the demand to make such ventures profitable enough to make them attractive. Moreover, the longer the period of time that ethnic groups reside in this country, the more acculturated they generally become. This also weakened the demand for the tangible products of their musical culture.

The 1970s and 1980s witnessed a strong movement toward multicultural perspectives in the arts, education, and humanities, a reawakened awareness that the United States is not a monolithic society. One minor result of this new assessment is the understanding that ethnic music plays some part in our cultural fabric. Since 1970, we have witnessed revitalization movements in klezmer, Native American, Hawaiian, and Norwegian American music among others. This music had been merely submerged by the commercial forces that shape our daily consciousness, bubbling along within the confines of its community.

Smithsonian Folkways has always included ethnic-American releases in its catalog. At Arhoolie, founder Chris Strachwitz's fondness for Spanish American music and the creolized forms from Louisiana and east Texas has ensured their places in his company's list. The bulk of the recording of ethnic music, however, has mainly been undertaken by small companies dedicated to meeting the needs of a narrowly targeted audience. As usually happens in our capitalist society, commercial companies spring up to fill the void left by major companies. In New York City, for example, the influx of Caribbean immigrants has created a thriving business for entrepreneurs hustling concerts and dances in addition to records and tapes. Canyon Records in New Mexico has been serving the Native American communities, albeit mostly Southwestern tribes, since the early 1960s. The documentation and marketing of popular and folk music of ethnic enclaves remains, even today, largely unknown outside of the communities themselves.

Our folk music heritage continues to interact with emerging popular genres; during the 1990s some very popular singer-songwriters, most notably Ani Di Franco, Tracy Chapman, Jim White, and The Dixie Chicks, all clearly bore the stamp of American folk music in their own work. The popular press continues to trace and help create new musical trends; the 1970s and 1980s brought alternative journals and magazines devoted to American vernacular music. Folk music publications such as *Living Blues, The Old Time Herald,* and other more ephemeral magazines have chronicled the history and development of vernacular music. Today, much information about these musics can be found on the thousands of Web sites (not all of them based in the United States) devoted to American vernacular music from Cajun to surf to tejano. Most of the noncommercial college and National Public Radio stations devote some of their weekly programming to folk music. And the attention paid to the revised *Anthology of*

O Brother!

Early in 2001, the Coen Brothers' film *O Brother Where Art Thou?* sparked the latest revival of interest in folk and folk-based film. A critical success, the movie's soundtrack has received almost as much attention as the film, selling more than six million copies as of early 2003. Most of the songs on *O Brother* are quiet, acoustic performances that draw on American folk music: "Hard Time Killing Floor Blues" (based on a 1931 performance by Skip James) and "O Death" are among its musical highlights. Although most of the songs were rotated into the mix on noncommercial public and college radio stations, there was at least one popular radio hit on the album: "I Am a Man of Constant Sorrow." In *O Brother* the song is played (in bluegrass style) by The Soggy Bottom Boys, and its video became part of the regular rotation on Country Music Television (CMT). In 2002, *O Brother* spawned a small industry of recordings and tours from Rounder Records' *O Sister! The Women's Bluegrass Collection,* to the highly successful Down from the Mountain mega-tour that featured folk and folk-based artists like Ricky Scaggs, The Fairfield Four, Allison Krauss and Union Station, Patty Loveless, and Ralph Stanley. If Stanley can gain national attention early in the twenty-first century, then who knows what folk musician's career will next be revived?

American Folk Music underscores the vitality of this music. These examples illustrate that a small, persistent, and formidable network of resources devoted to the preservation and dissemination of folk music exists.

THREE

Varieties of American Folk Music

B ecause American folk music is so eclectic and encompassing, it's not always entirely clear what
belongs under its umbrella. With its roots in gospel, blues,
and country, one could argue that rock 'n' roll might belong
in this chapter too. In this instance, tradition prevails, popular genres are eschewed, and the definition of what is folk
largely sticks with the "music that falls between the cracks"
idea (including genres such as bluegrass and western swing).
This chapter, however, includes several of the most interesting forms of regional folk music, such as chicken scratch and
fife and drum band, that may be unknown to most Americans
as folk music.

Ballad singing: Ballads tell a story, most often about love, betrayal, war, criminal acts, or natural disasters. You can think
of a ballad as an ultra-short story that leaps over the details to
linger on the more powerful and dramatic scenes. But even

the most climactic action unfolds in objective prose and even the most gruesome or emotional scenes are revealed dispassionately and without critical comment. They are often sung as though they were being recounted by a jaded court reporter who has heard it all dozens of times before.

Ballads were brought over from the British Isles as well as created anew in America. Older British ballads are often called *Child ballads,* after the late-nineteenth-century Harvard University english professor James Francis Child, who cataloged and organized several hundred of them. The Child ballads that survived into the twentieth century contain more universal themes with generalized plots, such as the lore about hard-hearted Barbara Allen or the roguish charm of Black Jack Davie. The hundreds that he omitted are called "broadsides" because they tended to be more journalistic, subjective, and topical. Most ballads of American origin, such as "The Titanic" and "Stackolee," come from the second half of the nineteenth or the early twentieth century. Ballad making in the United States was not dissimilar to the British broadside tradition, especially in its stereotyping of character and situation. Before the twentieth century, ballads were often sung a cappella, but today solo ballad singing is all but a lost art.

Ballads were often transmitted via aural tradition, but these songs were also written down in personal notebooks or for publication in limited edition, locally circulated chap books. Beginning in the 1920s, phonograph records helped keep some native American ballads in our minds and hearts. The Columbia Old-Time country series of the mid-1920s through the early 1930s, for example, included the cowboy ballads "Bandit Cole Younger" and "On the Old Chisholm Trail" among its releases. Though they sound very distant from postmodern America, some ballads, such as "John

Henry," have survived well into the twentieth century. Even in the post-rock era, ballads find their way into American popular culture. Gordon Lightfoot's hit song "The Wreck of the *Edmond Fitzgerald*" about a 1975 ship disaster on Lake Superior, provides one notable example. Throughout their long and interesting career, The Grateful Dead often performed a variant of "Casey Jones" (a song about a turn-of-the-last-century Tennessee train wreck) as part of their live gigs.

Bluegrass: Bluegrass emerged in the mid-1940s, and Bill Monroe is largely responsible for its genesis and dissemination. Based on previous genres as diverse as African American gospel quartet singing, and old-time string-band music, bluegrass is sometimes called *high-octane mountain music*. Its geographic roots lie in the fertile tristate area where Tennessee, Virginia, and North Carolina meet, which is home to pioneering bluegrass artists such as Curly King and The Tennessee Hill Toppers and The Stanley Brothers and their Clinch Mountain Boys. Bluegrass was quickly disseminated not only owing to live performances but through radio broadcasts and recordings on the postwar independent record companies that sprang up across the United States.

Bluegrass bands are characterized by high-tenor lead singing and an ensemble, including a five-string banjo, string bass, mandolin, fiddle, and guitar. Late in 1946, Earl Scruggs joined Bill Monroe, bringing his distinctive three-finger banjo roll to The Blue Grass Boys. This addition provided the band with the quintessential bluegrass instrumentation and performance styles. Their Columbia records from 1947 and 1948 are the first instantly recognizable bluegrass discs; *Mother's Only Sleeping* and *Blue Moon of Kentucky* remain two of the finest examples. In the ensuing five years, Monroe went on to record many traditional bluegrass tunes that are now recognized as classic performances of American music.

By 1950, this music could be heard across the South. Hundreds of bands were playing bluegrass, and its impact soon spread far beyond its hearth area, spilling across the entire South and into the Midwest. Surprisingly, the word *bluegrass* did not seem to have gained favor until the early to middle 1950s, when it began to be more universally applied to this music. No one knows exactly when this occurred, but by 1956 it was used in print. Within ten years, bluegrass had become part of the folk revival and had its own magazine (*Bluegrass Unlimited*), and the first bluegrass festival was staged near Roanoke, Virginia.

Today bluegrass musicians are found across the world. They play at festivals, record for both major and independent labels, and have spawned creative forms. Some particularly inventive musicians, like banjo player Bill Keith and guitarist Tony Rice, began in bluegrass and still perform bluegrass, but they developed groups that played new grass, progressive bluegrass, and even dawg music—a jazz-bluegrass fusion pioneered by David Grissman in the mid-1970s. Despite these changes, all bluegrass performers pay homage to their progenitor, the late Bill Monroe who remains the father of bluegrass.

Blues: Blues emerged as a distinctive style around the beginning of the twentieth century. The product of multigenesis in the Deep South (east Texas, Mississippi, Louisiana, and Alabama), blues was a synthesis of the traditions that preceded it: dance tunes, minstrel songs, secular ditties, and spirituals. Because of its origins, it is impossible to assign a specific date and geographical location for the first blues performance.

There are several reasons why blues developed at this time.

First, the period of Jim Crow racism added misery and hard times to the black community. Second was the more ready availability of mail-order guitars and their greater popularity among folk musicians. Guitars were perfect for black folk musicians because of their portability, the primary chords (one, four, five) were easy to play and because the strings easily bent to accommodate the sometimes flatted tonality commonly found in black folk music.

Early blues probably sounded similar to the rather free-form hollers sung as people worked hard in the fields and to the secular ditties popular during the 1880s and 1890s. Certainly the subjects would have been similar: mistreatment, money problems, and difficulty between the sexes. It took the blues tradition at least ten years to diffuse across the South and gain acceptability. Nonetheless, blues provided one of the most important creative outlets in response to increased repression and a renewal of hard times after the heady, progressive days of Reconstruction.

Blues are built on a series of rhymed couplets that speak the "truth" about life, one of the principal reasons why this new music appealed to its listeners. As the musician played the low-down music and sang about mutual concerns, blues promoted a dialogue between the musician and his or her audience. Because the early blues were played at house parties and dances rather than formal concert halls, audiences shouted encouragement and sometimes interacted with musicians by joining in the singing. Dancing, another means of releasing energy and frustration as well as creative movement, quickly became another important ingredient in this dialogue.

The first blues songs were almost certainly of variable length, probably between ten bars and fourteen bars. The standardization of the twelve-bar format appeared in sheet music as early as 1912. However, the twelve-bar blues form did not become codified for at least another decade; therefore, early blues musicians often played cycles of whatever bar length suited them. The length of early blues was probably determined by the words being sung. Blues singers demonstrated many musical characteristics that are regional in nature. The early downhome blues styles can be assigned to three general regions: the Southwest, mid-South, and Southeast.

Blues also exerted a strong influence on jazz, which emerged at about the same time. The impact of blues occurred in two ways. The first is the musical inflections, the bent notes, and the flatted seventh, in particular, which lend this music its characteristic sound. Second is the twelve-bar musical form itself that has informed jazz musicians from King Oliver to Wynton Marsalis.

Cajun: Eighteenth-century settlers to Louisiana from the maritime provinces of Canada brought with them their older French songs and dance music played on fiddles. They eventually picked up the keening, high-pitched vocal style of the indigenous Native Americans, which has become a trademark of the music. The African American residents contributed a slightly syncopated rhythmic sense and the concept of improvisational singing. Hispanic settlers introduced the guitar to the Cajuns, while white Americans provided them with new tunes. By the 1850s, most of the basic elements of this highly creolized music were in place.

In the nineteenth century, dances were usually held in homes on weekends with fiddles, sometimes in pairs, providing most of the music. The diatonic accordion, so well known in Cajun music today, was introduced into the area by German settlers who came to Texas in the 1840s and 1850s. The fiddles and accordions were soon joined together because they could be heard over the loud and raucous dances. By early in the twentieth century, small dance bands consisting of an accordion, fiddle, some percussion instrument (spoons, washboard, or triangle), and a guitar were found in dance halls all across the region. Cajuns danced to polkas, waltzes, and two-steps on weekend nights in small, rural dance halls lined with wooden benches under which their children slept while their parents danced the night away.

By the middle 1930s, The Hackberry Ramblers had synthesized Cajun music with the pioneering western swing sound and were among the first Cajun musicians to use amplified instruments. Electric steel guitars were soon heard in dance halls across southern Louisiana. These songs were now pushed forward by the drums that Cajun groups began using. At the front of this modernization of traditional Cajun music was Harry Choates, whose popularity ensured him jobs as far west as Waco, Texas.

The internal revitalization of Cajun folk music began slowly in the late 1940s. Led by the accordion-playing Iry Lejeune, the older songs once more began popping up at dances and on play lists of the local radio stations. Interest in Cajun music also increased during the early days of the folk revival. The 1964 Newport Folk Festival became the first major event at which Cajun musicians like Gladius Thibodeaux and Dewey Balfa were featured outside of its home. Today younger musicians such as Bruce Daigrepont, Zachary Richard, Michael Doucet, Steve Riley, Marc Savoy—along with an older generation that includes Tony Balfa and Nathan Menard—perform their indigenous music at folk festivals and clubs across America and Europe.

Chicken scratch: Contemporary chicken scratch, with its saxophone, accordion, and guitar ensemble, might be mistaken for a highly regional and idiosyncratic version of country and western music crossed with a polka band. This music, in fact, is strongly rooted in the Southwest's mix of Mexican, Indian, and European cultures. Chicken scratch (or waila, as it is also often referred to) is most often performed by members of The Tohono O'odham Tribe, whose nation is situated in southern Arizona just to the west of Tucson. Small ensembles of Tohono O'odham musicians, most often playing guitar and fiddle, performed for small events and local festivals as well as in Tucson from the mid-1800s on. The instrumentation used to provide waila music changed very little until the late 1940s, when the influence of conjunto music altered this line up. The guitars and fiddles were gradually augmented and often replaced by the standard norteno instrumentation of guitar, string bass, drums, button accordion, and, often, alto saxophone. The context for contemporary waila, which is ultimately derived from the Spanish word *baile* meaning "social dance," varies. It is heard at the wildly popular dances mostly held on the nation's lands and at weddings and birthday parties. But the most important context is the village feasts, held on a saint's day, which everyone from the youngest to the most elderly attends.

Conjunto: Conjunto is the best-known form of Tex-Mex music, one that is sometimes called musica norteno (music of the north), reflecting both its origins in northern Mexico and its importance in the United States. Norteno accordion playing probably began in the mid-nineteenth century as a solitary pursuit, with other instruments being added, perhaps as the demand for conjunto music for dancing increased. As its popularity grew, conjunto musicians gradually replaced the wind instruments and violins with the now ubiquitous bajo sexto (an oversize twelve-string guitar). During the 1920s through the 1940s, the two-row accordion was favored by the majority of musicians, most notably Santiago Jimenez of San Antonio and Narciso Martinez, who lived in the lower Rio Grande Valley. By the 1940s, this blue-collar-style of music had established itself as the most prominent form of folk music along the border. One of the many changes that followed the close of World War II was the move to the three-button accordions, which became a lead instrument as the bajo sexto and bass took over the majority of the rhythmic and harmonic functions. The drums were also added to many conjunto ensembles around this time, resulting in the now familiar four-piece band consisting of a small diatonic button accordion, acoustic bass, and bajo sexto. Contemporary conjunto is performed at bars, restaurants, festivals, or other public gatherings wherever Mexican Americans live.

Corridos: Like Native American and Child ballads, corridos tell a highly dramatic story. The greatest and lengthiest cycle of corridos are set along the border Texas and Mexico over an eighty-year period between about 1850 and 1930. Many of these recount the long-standing struggle for civil rights and social justice and are clear precursors for the Chicano movement. After 1930, the number and importance of border ballads diminished and their topics expanded. During World War II, for example, corridos about war heroes and conflicts emerged. After the assassination of John F. Kennedy in 1963, corridos about the fallen president flooded the marketplace. Fulfilling the role carried out by spirituals during the black American civil rights movement, corridos served the Chicano movement during its emerging years. For example, tunes celebrating his heroic efforts to help organize farm workers in California and to boycott grapes during the late 1960s and into the 1970s were composed for Cesar Chavez. In the mid-

1990s another cycle of corridos about the political and social struggles of Indians in the southern Mexican state of Chiapus emerged during the middle of the conflict itself. As narco-trafficing increased along the border during the 1990s, a rash of corridos about drug dealers also increased.

Cowboy songs: Cowboy songs describe the daily life and, quite often, the work of the cowboy. The early cowboy singers (from the late nineteenth into the twentieth century) represent a musical genre unto themselves. Montana, Idaho, Wyoming, New Mexico, and the other western states were largely the domain of first- or second-generation pioneers. Such songs were first written and sung by cowboys as they drove cattle, mended fences, branded calves, and handled other related ranch work. By the 1890s cowboy songs such as "When the Work's All Done This Fall" and "The Last Great Round-Up" began showing up in newspapers and magazines, often as a poem or a broadside, or in songbooks. They often appeared as ballads whose structure and melodies owed much to contemporary folk and popular tunes. Cowboys lived, worked, and performed music in a world quite separate from the country music that developed in the Southeast and Midwest.

Gene Autry, with songs that he popularized on the silver screen such as "Back in the Saddle Again" and "Riding down the Canyon," initially mythologized and romanticized cowboys by way of the electronic media. Autry's early career included a stint as a musician and comedian with Fields Brothers Marvelous Medicine Show and a relief telegraph operator. In 1929, he traveled to New York City for his first recording session, beginning a career that included dozens of grade B western movies in the mid-1930s. Autry helped open the gates for others to follow and solidified the connection between country music and western themes and images that continue to this day in the work of Michael Allen Murphy, Guy Clark, Mike Williams, and Chris Le Doux, a few of whom actually worked as full-time cowboys in addition to their careers as singers. The contemporary cowboy poetry gatherings held annually in Nevada and Utah represent another modern manifestation of this nineteenth-century tradition.

Fife and Drum Bands: Fife and drum band music is perhaps the best example of a regional style of black American folk music. This music evolved from the military tradition and became transformed by black musicians after the Civil War into the twentieth century. The music itself was played on two primary instruments, drums and cane fifes, constituting a small ensemble. Two snare drums and a bass drum constitute the drum section, and the cane fife is homemade.

Once a tradition that existed in several sections of the South, by the turn of the twentieth century, African American fife and drum bands were largely confined to the deep middle South. Northern Mississippi remains about the only place that fife and drum band music is still performed. The major summer holidays—Memorial Day, Fourth of July, and Labor Day—provide the context for performing this music, a legacy of its military and patriotic heritage. Picnics featuring barbecued goat and plenty of liquor begin in the afternoon and run well into the night, while the fife and drum bands play and people march behind or dance to the music.

Gospel: Gospel is another of those encompassing genres that has different meanings, depending on the context. Gospel is always sacred music; it's also part of white American and African American musical culture or, as is often the case, a mixture of both. Sanctified music, also called "holiness singing," crosses racial boundaries and is associated with the various Pentecostal churches found throughout the United States. This entry, however, focuses on African American traditions, whereas the Southern gospel covers the white American material.

Gospel refers to both composed and more traditional music. Spirituals are a prime example of traditional African American gospel music. Even though most spirituals originated in the era before the Civil War, a surprising number of them is still performed today. It's not uncommon for songs such as "Glory, Glory, Hallelujah (When I Lay My Burden Down)" or "Rollin' Through an Unfriendly Land" to be heard at rural churches or performed by a gospel quartet. In some instances, spirituals are performed a cappella, but this performance practice is less common today. In other instances, some of these older, traditional songs are heard in new settings, perhaps sung by a mass choir.

Lyrics written and published by African American gospel composers first circulated at the end of the nineteenth century, and Philadelphia's Albert Tindley was among the pioneers. The best-known gospel composer, however, is the Reverend Thomas A. Dorsey, a former blues singer and pianist who turned exclusively to sacred music in the early 1930s. He wrote "Precious Lord," "Peace in the Valley," and scores of other selections, which are so well known that many people assume they are far older and part of the public domain. Dorsey, along with Memphis residents the Reverend Herbert Brewster and Lucie Campbell, furthered what was a radical movement in the 1930s but that is now considered to be old-line and conservative.

Even today's most progressive gospel music has strong roots in folk practices, which can take many forms. For example, mass choirs (which have been popular since the 1960s) usually perform a repertoire that mixes newly composed material with traditional songs. The practices of modern gospel singers look back not only to older singers like Willie Mae Ford Smith or Brother Joe May but also to the vocal slides, moans, and ornamentations that were sung in field hollers. Finally, such well-known techniques as antiphony (call and response) often bond the singers together with the members of the congregation in a musical and spiritual dialogue.

Klezmer: Brought to the United States by professional musicians from eastern Europe, many of whom migrated here between 1880 and 1920, klezmer refers to the instrumental dance music played by small instrumental ensembles. The word *klezmer* is a Yiddish term that contracts the Hebrew words *kley* and *zmer,* which can be translated as "vessel of melody" or "musician." In Europe, most of these itinerant musicians were part of an economic and social underclass who made their living performing for weddings, weekend dances, and other celebrations. In this regard, the early blues musicians who played in the rural South during the 1920s and 1930s held much the same social position as klezmer musicians. Because klezmer musicians played at so many different types of venues, they soon developed a wide repertoire that favored both dances (waltzes, horas, polkas, and mazurkas) as well as lyrical styles, especially the doina (an improvised melody and song rooted in the tradition of Romanian shepherds). The instrumental music was gradually augmented by a singer or poet or social commentator who vocalized about the events of the day. These "badkhn," as they came to be known, served as purveyors of news and information and sometimes satirized members of the audience, public officials, or current events.

Twentieth-century klezmer combines elements of folk and

popular music filtered through the Romanian, Hungarian, Bulgarian, and Russian styles found in eastern Europe into a unique blend. The music thrived not only in big cities like New York and Chicago but also in the summer Catskill resorts from about 1910 through the 1950s. Commercial recordings of klezmer bands led by Dave Tarras, Abe Schwartz, and others were popular until its appeal to a younger audience diminished. Klezmer's nadir came during the 1960s and 1970s when the aging of the first and even the second generation of musicians left a void. By the 1980s, however, klezmer was revitalized by younger musicians like Hankus Netsky, Henry Sapoznik, and Andy Statman who also sparked a renewed interest in this unique aspect of Jewish expressive culture. Today there are scores of klezmer bands, with names like The New Orleans Klezmer All Stars and Klezmer Plus, performing nationwide.

Mariachi: Mariachi is a folk-based music that remained a regional style of music until the first decade of the twentieth century. In its more down-home settings—both in Mexico and the United States—this music is performed at family or community events such as birthdays, cookouts, wedding anniversaries, and neighborhood festivals. Mariachi musicians also perform for audiences at cafés or occasionally on street corners for anyone who will meet their fees. Contemporary mariachi music has its roots in Mexico in the 1930s, making it roughly the same age as bluegrass. Today mariachi almost always refers to an ensemble of between five and ten players that combine fiddles, trumpets, and guitars with two stringed instruments, the vihuela and guitarron, which are less familiar to most citizens of the United States. The instrumentalists typically also sing, and most of the songs are performed in Spanish. For many Americans mariachi is *the* quintessential form of Mexican and, by extension, Mexican American music.

Mele: Several types of vocal music could be heard in Hawaii, but the mele (a chant with Polynesian roots) remains the most important. Soloists predominate in traditional Hawaiian chanting. Those who could please their listeners with a sustained unbroken performance were most sought after. Secondarily, a chanter should excel at prolonging and controlling vowel fluctuation and changing his or her tone through manipulation of the chest muscles. Mele are usually narratives commenting on religion, historical events, or societal issues.

The widely recognized hula actually refers to a dance that interprets a mele. Due both to increasing urbanization and to shifting tastes, the older style of hula that interprets animal life has almost disappeared from the Hawaiian repertoire. Hulas can be performed sitting down or standing up. But in either case, the complicated gestures are keyed to words or phrases in the mele. Hula mele are rather formalized into contrasting sections, often *a-b-c-b-c-b-c-d*, to make them easier to follow. Seated hulas are often accompanied by body percussion or some sort of instrument, whereas standing hulas are generally augmented by at least one percussionist-chanter. At least two mele, *oli* and *kepakepa*, are strictly chanted traditions that are never interpreted by a hula.

Aside from the guitar, most of Hawaii's folk instruments are percussive, and the majority of them are affiliated with hula mele. For example the pahu hula is a wooden drum made from a hollow log, and its use is limited to accompany the hula pahu (hula dance). Other drums are made from indigenous material such as coconut shells (puniu). Rattles made of various indigenous gourds constitute the other important form of

Hawaiian percussive instrument. Even beating wooden sticks together (kala'au) can accompany this dancing and singing.

Polka music: Although the polka is a dance set to 2/4 beat, *polka music* is a term used to describe musical cultures largely promulgated by musicians of northern European descent. In Europe the polka was viewed as low-class, boisterous, and deemed dangerous to polite society. In the United States, the Midwest served as polka's epicenter because so many northern Europeans immigrated there in the last half of the nineteenth century.

Even in early 2000, Midwestern polka music remained identified with specific ethnic groups. Because it has been over 100 years since most of these northern Europeans have immigrated to the United States, today's polka music and dance is distinctly American. And, despite the ethnic pride displayed in names such as Karl and the Country Dutchmen and Norm Dombrowski's Happy Notes, there has been considerable musical interaction among these musicians of German, eastern European, and Scandinavian heritage.

Nonetheless, enough differences remain—especially in instrumentation—that you can discern some important differences, which are related to the instrumentation of bands, their musical repertoire, and their national or regional origins. This is perhaps most easily noted in their choice of instruments. The contemporary Polish American style, which is particularly strong in Chicago and Milwaukee, highlights reed and brass instruments (most often clarinets and trumpets). Their German (Dutchmen) and Czech neighbors favor similar line ups but often add a tuba or sousaphone to the ensemble, giving these bands an even richer sound. Polka musicians of Slovenian heritage favor an accordion over concertina, whereas Norwegian American polka bands are more likely to feature a fiddle in their line up. These may appear to be subtle distinctions, but they are important not only to the musicians themselves but also in the overall sound of each tradition.

Powwows: Although Native American music is not monolithic, and regional variations are still heard, in modern times many Native Americans have unified into a pan-Indian movement. The general concept of such gatherings, called powwows, is not new; American Indians have come together to celebrate such tribal functions as harvesting for centuries. But beginning in the late nineteenth century, the idea of a gathering across tribal lines began to gain favor, and powwows are the most well known public gathering of Indians in the United States.

Powwows are usually held in the summertime and are most commonly staged in the plains and Northwest, but now can be found from Maine to California and from Texas through North Dakota. The name for these weekend events derived from an Algonquin term referring to a healing ceremony. In the early twentieth-first century the name has been applied to a gathering involving socializing, food ways, and spiritual enlightenment. Arts and crafts are also sold, partly for cultural reasons but also for tribal fund-raising.

Music and dance are central to powwows. The singing is dominated by males who usually sing in unison to the accompaniment of a single large bass drum. The dancers usually wear ornate and often highly symbolic regalia. Regional and specialized tribal dances are sometimes held in addition to the commonly practiced round dances. Over the past twenty years, there has been a movement to increase unique tribal customs, such as the inclusion of games like lacrosse or gambling hand games, within pan-Indian powwows, because of the clear danger of homogenization. Such local or tribal variations might seem minor to the casual observer but they help differentiate the cultures.

Protest songs: The encompassing term *Protest Songs* is most often associated with politically oriented songs written by folk-based singers, such as Phil Ochs and Bob Dylan, in the 1960s. These songs often commented on contemporary topics like the Vietnam War and civil rights for African Americans. But protest songs also include other areas, like topical songs and freedom songs, and existed long before the folk revival. In the late nineteenth and early twentieth centuries, people used protest songs to denounce slavery, promote women's suffrage, and organize workers in labor unions. Protest singers often put new words to existing familiar tunes.

Though not synonymous, topical songs are closely related to protest songs. Topical songs focus on a particular event or place, such as a coal mining disaster or the plight of textile mill workers, without necessarily protesting overtly. Many topical songs imply problems or issues that deserve closer scrutiny without directly stating the problems. Woody Guthrie's songs about the Dust Bowl along with the "Grand Coulee Dam," and the "1913 Strike" represent a mixture of topical and protest songs as do many of the coal mining songs performed by Aunt Molly Jackson, Florence Reese, and Sarah Ogan Gunning (proto-feminists all) in the 1930s and 1940s.

Freedom songs are African American protest songs, most of which are closely linked with sacred traditions. African American slaves often sang about freedom and (veiled) protest, using careful wording to avoid arousing the suspicion of the slave owners. A spiritual like "Go Down Moses" related a biblical story, yet its refrain "Let my people go!" certainly could be applied to the situation of the African American slaves too. Other songs, like "Follow the Drinkin' Gourd," were simply coded instructions to help slaves escape to freedom. Spirituals, often overt protest songs, were widely used during the civil rights movement. Folk-gospel singer Odetta, opera singer Marian Anderson, gospel singer Mahalia Jackson, and pop star Harry Belafonte all sang for their own struggle for civil rights during the 1963 March on Washington, using "Oh, Freedom" and "I Shall Not Be Moved" to relate their message.

Protest singing gained its widest currency in the 1960s when Pete Seeger, Joan Baez, and others used this medium to convey a message against the Vietnam War. Other topics for protest by left-wing folk-based singers in the 1960s and 1970s included nuclear weapons, American imperialism abroad, and women's rights. Protest songs are a mainstay of folk-based singers and are ingrained in American folk and popular culture. As recently as the fall of 2001, "We Shall Overcome" (a longtime favorite of union organizers and the civil rights movement) rang out over Yankee Stadium for a ceremony commemorating the terrorist attacks of September 11, 2001.

Shape-note singing: The first widely recognized form of white religious folk music was found in the shape-note tune books published in the early 1800s. The shapes themselves represent a simplified system (called fasola, referring to the last three syllables used in sight singing—fa, sol, and la) to help people who were not conversant with standard western notation. It is also known as sacred harp singing because of the very popular book *The Sacred Harp*, a recent edition of which was published in 1991. The appearance of anthems and fuguing tunes by American composers drawn from oral tradition further establishes its folk roots and can be found in the first Southern tune book compiled by Ananias Davidson, *Kentucky Harmony* (1816).

The tunes are presented in four-part harmony with the

main melody given to the tenor voices. The voices are unusually independent, marking a move away from the harmonizing of a melody so commonly found during this time. The tunes themselves (the melody lines) often came from broadside ballads, fiddle pieces, or popular songs of the day, which the tune book compilers reworked rather than created. They are written in a mixture of major and minor keys, with some modal tunes occurring also. Although such tunes did have some parallels in eighteenth- and nineteenth-century hymnody, these writers undeniably created a distinctive sound that would seem a bit unruly to those trained in the standard European classical music.

Shape-note singing is, above all, a social form of religious music. The singing school teachers brought people together to instruct them in the rudiments of the four-note (later back to the seven-note) system. People also gathered in small and large groups for the express purpose of singing this music. By the late 1800s, formal singing conventions were being held across the South. These lasted for varying lengths of time, from an afternoon to several days, depending on the gathering's size and the distance people had to travel. The singers sat in sections arranged by the distribution of the four voices. A different singer often led each song, which is first sung with the syllables to familiarize everyone and then with the words.

Contemporary folk shape-note singing (mostly but not entirely among white Southerners) continues today, with its strongest following in Alabama and Georgia. With song leaders and singing school teachers such as Hugh McGraw of northern Georgia and Helen Nance Church of Yadkin County, North Carolina, spreading the word, the tradition has remained alive. Although it has never disappeared from our cultural landscape, this style of singing has undergone something of a renaissance over the past thirty years. There are now many other revival groups across the country, including in New England, where this type of singing went largely unheard during its days of greatest popularity.

Southern gospel music: Southern gospel is not a single style of music but covers a broad range of conservative white Christian music with a biblical message. The roots of southern gospel, which took shape in the southeast part of the United States in the 1920s, range from African American spirituals to the songs and anthems published in late-nineteenth-century shape-note hymn books. The music emerged from its rural southern enclave by way of radio broadcasts, commercial recordings, and live performances, illustrating the ongoing interaction between folk and popular culture.

Southern gospel music is performed by a wide range of groups, such as soloists, small family groups, guitar-accompanied evangelists, and, most notably, quartets. In the 1910s and 1920s, music publishers like Vaughan and Stamps-Baxter sponsored traveling quartets that helped promote their songbooks. By the late 1940s, groups such as The Blackwood Brothers and Statesmen Quartet emerged and soon became among the most popular and influential southern gospel quartets. At the height of their popularity in the mid-1950s, these quartets sang to packed venues, recorded regularly, and had syndicated radio broadcasts that brought their message of Christian salvation across the United States.

Western swing: Long a cultural crossroads, Texas birthed western swing in the 1930s. This genre looked toward the string-bands and norteno music of Mexico, the Cajun of Louisiana, and the German American communities of the hill country near Austin and San Antonio. From black musicians came blues and jazz. Combine these influences with cowboy songs and fiddle tunes and you get western swing.

Bob Wills remains the undisputed king of this genre. By 1931 the Wills Fiddle Band became known as the Light Crust Doughboys, named in honor of their radio sponsor—Light Crust Dough. The band slowly expanded its size and scope, along with its local popularity. Bob Wills and his Texas Playboys, complete with string bass, tenor banjo, and piano, became their new name in 1933. The mid-1930s repertoire of Bob Wills and his Texas Playboys reveals the breadth of western swing's most influential band. Their 1935 and 1936 ARC (Columbia) records demonstrate their catholic approach to music: "I Can't Give You Anything but Love," "Oklahoma Rag," "Just Friends," "Mexicali Rose," "There's a Quaker Girl in Old Quaker Town," and "Get Along Home Cindy." But above all were their interpretations of black blues, especially the light-hearted double-entendre songs taken from records by Tampa Red, Big Bill, Frankie Jaxon, Memphis Minnie, and others: "Fan It," "No Matter How She Done It," "What's the Matter with the Mill?," and "Sitting on Top of the World."

By the late 1930s the more free-spirited western swing bands included a complement of horn and reed players in the groups. Inspired by the success of Tommy Dorsey, Benny Goodman, and Glenn Miller, western swing bands began using jazz-influenced musicians who soloed over the pulsing 2/4 meter provided by the rhythm section. Only Texas in the 1930s could produce bands such as Adolph Hopner's, led by an accordion playing Czech American. Another San Antonio band, The Tune Wranglers, recorded popular tunes such as "Texas Sand," which further solidified the importance of Texas nationalism in this music that remains to this day.

Western swing remains popular in Texas and Wills's name remains magical in Texas, even thirty years after his death.

Work song: A work song is simply any song performed by workers that assists them in carrying out their task. With the exception of sea chanties and possibly some nineteenth-century cowboy songs, work songs have been principally the domain of black American laborers, who sang them to accompany everything from shoe shining to poling river boats. Work songs fulfill two basic functions. One is to pass the time while workers carry out monotonous, repetitive jobs such as hoeing a row of cotton, chopping or pulling weeds, caulking a boat's hull, or loading a truck. The second is to co-ordinate jobs that demand split-second group efforts such as driving spikes or lining railroad tracks.

Work songs, which are constructed of short and repetitive phrases, also provide the singers with a sense of solidarity by participating in a communal act. The singing gives workers a greater measure of control, co-opting that role from their boss or overseer. Finally, work songs relieved tension by allowing blacks to complain about their living conditions and treatment by their employers or overseers. Today, even in prisons, work songs have all but disappeared largely due to mechanization.

Zydeco: This unique regional music is closely related to Cajun music and is most simply described as creolized African American Cajun music. Traditional zydeco music and its performance contexts are very similar to its white counterparts. Found primarily in venues that stretch west from Lafayette to Houston, zydeco has developed since Reconstruction. Whether the musicians favor the older Cajun sound or prefer the blues or soul-tinged music, it is all propelled forward by a rhythmic drive and syncopation that betrays its African-Caribbean background.

The black Americans of southwestern Louisiana are truly creoles because they are a mixture of African, French, and Spanish descent. The music they play became known as zydeco, a creolized form of the French word for "snapbeans"—local residents often say that it is derived from an old Southwestern Louisiana dance tune known as "Les Haricots Sont Pas Sales" (The snapbeans are not salted). Zydeco refers not only to music but also to the event where the dancing and music takes place. Thus one can host a zydeco, which includes music, food, dancing, and socializing. Especially popular are zydecos held at a fais-do-do, an informal house party where the music and dancing last far into the night.

Clifton Chenier was the best-known zydeco musician. Before passing away from kidney disease in 1984 he toured extensively, bringing his modern zydeco music to large concert halls and small dance halls across the country. Chenier transformed zydeco music by using his larger piano-keyed accordion and incorporating elements of blues and rock 'n' roll. His band usually included a sax and full rhythm section in addition to his brother Cleveland's washboard.

Since the 1980s the impact of zydeco has grown to international proportions. The amplified blues-based bands of Nathan and The Zydeco Cha Chas, Terence Semien, Beau Jocque, Queen Ida and The Bon Ton Zydeco Band, and Buckwheat Zydeco have toured Europe and played at music festivals across the United States. Nonetheless, many zydeco musicians continue to perform for local weekly dances in their southwestern Louisiana or southeastern Texas hometowns.

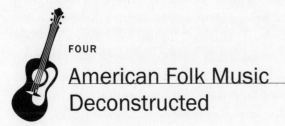

FOUR

American Folk Music Deconstructed

olk music casts a wide net, encompassing styles as musically and geographically disparate as chicken scratch, blues, and ballad singing. Text and instruments are the essential elements of American folk music, and they can be combined in myriad ways. Today, ballad singing often has instrumental accompaniment, but a hundred years ago many ballads were sung a cappella. Blues piano players usually sing but they also include a few flashy instrumental pieces as part of their repertoire. Chicken scratch is largely an instrumental tradition in which singing occupies a secondary role.

With these musical and culture changes altering the nature of vernacular American music, can there still be folk musicians in the early twenty-first century? Yes, even though it is perhaps increasingly difficult. Take accordion-playing Santiago Jimenez Jr. as one example. Born in San Antonio, Texas, in 1944, his father pioneered the modern style of conjunto

(Tex-Mex) musician in the 1930s through the 1950s. His older brother Flaco is an internationally recognized master of the accordion. Jimenez performs his distinctive music throughout Texas and has recorded scores of records for small regional and major independent labels, such as Arhoolie and Rounder, over the years. Although his older rancheros, polkas, and waltzes may sound wildly outdated or even alien to ears raised on Selena, Ricky Martin, and Julio Iglesius, Santiago Jimenez has already helped inspire a generation of musicians born in the 1960s and 1970s. These new kings and queens of conjunto will be carrying on this tradition (albeit always morphing into something slightly different, of course) well into the present century. Conjunto's roots, nonetheless, will be evident to anyone listening.

That the Jimenez family favors the accordion underscores the fact that American folk musicians use a wide variety of instruments. Well-known instruments ranging from guitars to fiddles are used by folk musicians, but they also perform on such less common instruments such as dulcimers, one-string diddley bows, and washboards. The use of particular instruments, not surprisingly, depends partially on regional or ethnic background as well as personal preference and family traditions. Some of them have surprisingly long histories that sometimes cross continents and many decades. Most of these instruments are acoustic models, although electrification and amplification have become increasingly common since World War II.

Because American folk music is multifaceted, it's useful to examine half a dozen of the common traits that tie these genres together and help understand and clarify their underlying elements. Whether you play old-time Bohemian polka music in Wisconsin; sing at a conservative African American Pentecostal church in Phoenix, Arizona; or are an active member of the D.C. Blues Society, these six traits will apply in some degree. They are meant to help describe the general themes that unify, rather than define, folk music in the United States.

Space and Time

Generally, folk music changes relatively little over time but a great deal as it travels over space. The religious folk song, "I'll Fly Away" (published by Albert Brumley in 1932 but often transmitted aurally), immediately became integrated into the repertoire of southern gospel groups as well as black gospel singers since its publication. Its heartfelt straightforward lyrics have remained constant over the decades, but the way it's performed depends on where you live and your ethnic background. A performance of "I'll Fly Away" by a southern gospel group in northern Virginia, for example, sounds quite different from a performance by an Hispanic American Pentecostal group from southern California. Lyrical innovations, in particular, are relatively rare in religious folk songs because its forms are largely performed within a conservative musical culture.

Community

American folk music is tied to specific communities. Such communities are found throughout the United States, and they are associated by way of their occupation, tribal affiliation, ethnic identity, or even physical proximity. Examples include Cajuns in southwestern Louisiana, French-speaking Maine lumberjacks, and Salvadorians living in Washington, D.C. These communities share characteristics such as speech patterns, food preferences, and names. Folk music is also often associated with even more casual or informal communities, such as the people who gather each Saturday evening for a pot luck followed by a contra dance in Windsor, Vermont, or a monthly sacred harp sing in Dothan, Alabama.

Authorship

Unlike most popular music, the origins of particular folk songs and tunes are generally unknown. We rarely know who writes folk songs or tunes. The authorship of country dance tunes such as "Round Town Gals" or "Mississippi Sawyer" is unknown, and versions can be heard in most sections of the United States. Specific songs, nonetheless, can sometimes be attributed to one region of the country or a particular folk community. "Walking Blues," for instance, clearly emanates from the Mississippi Delta blues tradition and likely developed as a particular song in the 1920s. Unlike most classical compositions and modern popular music, the authorship of most folk songs remains anonymous.

Dissemination

Despite the fact that you sometimes hear folk music on the radio and on recordings, it's often disseminated informally by word of mouth or aurally. Folk music is learned within a community by people who either grow up in or become integrated into a particular community. The folk process rarely entails formal lessons or classes. Conservatories and college music departments almost never offer "Field Holler 101" or "How to Play Fiddle Lithuanian Style" as part of their curriculum. Instead, folk music is usually integrated into everyday life, and it is learned so musicians can participate in a part of worship, relaxation, or social activity. Since the 1920s, folk and folk-based music has also been disseminated by way of radio, recordings, television, film, and the Internet.

Professionalism

Although you will find a handful of musicians who earn a living from their music, such as Chicago blues man Muddy Waters, who performed an electrified version of Mississippi Delta blues that formed the basis for rock 'n' roll, folk music is most often performed by nonprofessionals. A small number of people make their full-time living from performing folk or folk-based music, most of whom came of age following the folk revival of the 1960s. Some exceptions include handicapped musicians, such as North Carolina–based blues man Blind Boy Fuller, and a few well-known individuals, like bluegrass mandolinist and progenitor Bill Monroe, who earned a full-time salary from performing a popularized form of folk music. The network of folk music performers largely consists of part-time musicians who play for others within their community. This would include the members of a down-home bluegrass band that regularly provides the music for the Saturday night dance at the Danville, Kentucky, VFW hall and for their Pentecostal Church on Sunday morning.

Musical Forms

Short forms and predictable patterns are essential elements in American folk music. Most American folk music falls into repetitive paradigms that are generally familiar to members of the community. Blues, for instance, tends to follow the same, basic harmonic progression based on one, four, five chords; however, its form invites individual or group improvisation within these well-established harmonic boundaries. While its forms are usually not complex, folk music is rarely simple. Just listen to the complex finger-picking guitar technique used by the Reverend Gary Davis, an African American and former blues man from North Carolina, if you think that folk music is easy to play!

FIVE

The Performers

The performers of American folk music are so numerous that their biographical sketches could fill this entire book. Picking the artists and groups to include here was not an easy task. The folks included in this chapter are influential in establishing a particular genre, such as Bill Monroe and bluegrass, important as leaders within their musical community, such as Dewey Williams and African American shape-note singing, typical of the genre, such as cowboy singer Brownie Ford, or have had national impact, such as Bob Dylan. They range from the relatively obscure, such as Bohemian American concertina legend "Whoopie John" Whilfarht to a household name like Woody Guthrie. All together, however, they provide a sound overview of the figures that make up American folk music.

Joan Baez (b. 1941): A leading figure in the folk revival and a public figure in the civil rights and free speak movements,

Baez spent her early years in Redlands, California, before her family moved to Boston near the end of Baez's high school career. By this time she was involved with music as a singer in her high school choir and as a guitarist. Baez enrolled in Boston University, where she studied drama. Already well known at local coffee houses, she began performing up and down the East Coast and soon dropped out of college.

In 1959, Baez appeared at the Newport Folk Festival, exposing her to a far wider audience and earning her a recording contract with the fledgling Vanguard Records. Not surprisingly, Vanguard quickly released a live recording of her Newport show, followed closely by the 1960 release of *Joan Baez*, which is rife with traditional material such as the British broadsides "John Riley" and "House of the Rising Sun." Baez continued to tour regularly, caught up in the folk boom, but it wasn't until the 1961 release of *Joan Baez, Vol. 2* that her career began to focus on human and civil rights. This identification was cemented in 1963 when Baez shared the stage at the historical March on Washington with Bob Dylan, Mahalia Jackson, and Martin Luther King Jr. As Baez became more politically active, her musical focus shifted and concentrated more on material that contained social commentary. Baez was also associated with causes like the free speech movement at Berkeley in 1964.

As the sixties progressed and the British Invasion drew folk fans to pop music, Baez (as well as Judy Collins and Bob Dylan) began to involve a variety of instruments and expanded orchestrations not generally associated with folk music to accompany her songs. In addition to leaning more toward pop music, she married antiwar protest leader and country music fan David Harris. In 1971, Baez released *Blessed Are . . .* , a double album that debuted "The Night

They Drove Old Dixie Down" and was the subject of a documentary film, *Carry It On,* about her life and career.

Throughout the 1970s, Baez continued to develop her own songwriting and touring, and enjoyed some mild success in the pop world. During the 1980s, she recorded very little in the United States until 1987 when the album *Diamonds & Rust* scored both a commercial and artistic success. Since then Baez has continued to mix contemporary songs (both her own and songs written by others) with some older traditional material in her concerts and on record.

DeFord Bailey (1899–1982): Long overlooked by folk music enthusiasts but recognized as the first African American star of the Grand Ole Opry, Bailey was born in 1899 in Carthage, Smith County, Tennessee, just east of Nashville. Stricken with infantile paralysis at the age of three years, Bailey recovered but had a deformed back and never grew taller than four feet, ten inches. However, he picked up the harmonica during this extended illness and emerged with a passion for music and the means by which to make a living. Bailey's youth was spent around the rural communities of Newsom and Thompson, where a railroad ran nearby. It was at the train stations that Bailey become fond of the sound of trains and composed tunes such as the highly evocative "Pan American Express." Bailey eventually joined his family in Nashville, where they had moved in search of employment. On December 6, 1925, he won second place with his performance of the minstrel show song "It Ain't Gonna Rain No More" held on radio station WDAD. Early in 1926, Bailey overcame the racial opposition of the station's manager and made his initial appearance on WSM Radio.

Bailey, known as the "Harmonica Wizard," became a regular

on the *WSM Barn Dance*, which was almost immediately renamed *The Grand Ole Opry*. Bailey eventually toured with other stars of the Opry, including Roy Acuff, Uncle Dave Macon, and Bill Monroe. Traveling throughout the South during the 1930s and 1940s presented interesting challenges; on some occasions either he posed as a baggage boy for the white performers or pretended to be Uncle Dave Macon's valet in order to get a room. In 1927 he began a brief recording career that lasted several years and included brief stints for Brunswick and Columbia.

Baily stayed with the Opry for fifteen years, but by 1941 he was forced off the show and began a thirty-year career of shining shoes at his shop on Twelfth Avenue South in Nashville. During the civil rights movement of the 1960s, Bailey's career rebounded. He appeared on a local syndicated blues television show, *Night Train*, and in 1965, he made a rare concert appearance at Vanderbilt University. He appeared on the Opry's old-timers show in 1974 at the Ryman Auditorium and again later that year to celebrate his seventy-fifth birthday. The year after Bailey's death on July 2, 1982, the Country Music Association recognized his achievements with a plaque and a monument at his gravesite.

Dewey Balfa (1927–1992): Born into a large musical family from Bayou Grand Louis near Mamou, Louisiana, Balfa's father, grandfather, and great-grandfather were all fiddlers. Balfa (and his older brother, Will) began playing fiddle as a child, and as a young man started a band with his brothers. The Balfa Brothers became known for their compelling twin fiddle sound, aching vocals, often performing with local accordion players such as Nathan Abshire, Hadley Fontenot, and Marc Savoy. At least two of their songs—"Pointe aux Pains" and "Parlez Nous á Boire"—have become standards among Cajun musicians. Despite their success the Balfas never played full time; Dewey, for example, worked at various times as a farmer, disc jockey, insurance salesman, and school bus driver.

The 1964 Newport Folk Festival (at which Balfa performed) helped awaken awareness of Cajun music outside of Louisiana and southeast Texas. Transformed by this experience, Balfa returned to Louisiana and worked tirelessly promoting Cajun music to audiences throughout North America, Europe, and Japan, recording albums for Swallow and Rounder, and appearing at local schools. He continued to play with his brothers until Will and guitarist Rodney died in a 1978 car accident. Dewey continued to perform with other family members, receiving the National Endowment for the Arts National Heritage Fellowship (1982) before his death in 1992.

Dock Boggs (1898–1964): Were it not for the folk revival of the early 1960s, Boggs would have almost certainly remained one of the fascinating highly original hillbillies who recorded in the late 1920s. His dozen recordings from 1927 to 1929, most notably "Danville Girl," "Pretty Polly," and "Country Blues," remain important examples of regional folk music. Born near Norton, Virginia, Boggs was the youngest of ten children and a coal miner by the age of twelve. He also picked up the banjo around the same time, choosing bluesy picking over the clawhammer style that surrounded him.

His big break finally came in 1927, when he successfully auditioned for executives from the Brunswick label, who sent him to New York City to record. Although they were artistically successful, their sales were modest and Brunswick did not invite him back for another session. Instead Boggs remained in southwestern Virginia, recording four songs for local entrepreneur W. E. Myer's local Lonesome Ace label in 1929. Hampered by poor distribution and dogged by the Depression, these records sold very poorly. Boggs continued to perform around the region until the early 1930s, however, until he returned to a job in the mines, where he worked until 1954, when mechanical innovations forced him out of a job.

In 1963, folk song collector and musician Mike Seeger located Boggs in Norton and convinced him that there was renewed interest in his music. Several months after meeting Seeger, Boggs performed at the American Folk Festival in Asheville, North Carolina. This was followed by stints at other folk festivals as well as a detailed series of recordings that appeared on Folkways. Ironically, Boggs has become even better known after his death in 1971. In 1997, the reworked Harry Smith's Anthology of American Folk Music won several Grammys and brought renewed interest in Bogg's music. Shortly thereafter the Revenant label released *Complete Early Recordings (1927–1929)*, followed by a Smithsonian/Folkways retrospective of his career. Boggs was the focus of a November 1998 *Atlantic Monthly* feature, "Cornbread When I'm Hungry," which discussed his life, career, and impact on twentieth-century American music.

The Carter Family (1925–1941): Arguably the most influential group in country music history, The Carter Family initially consisted of A.P. and Sara. Born and raised in the Clinch Mountains of Virginia, Alvin Pleasant Delaney Carter (1891–1960) learned to play fiddle as a child, with his mother teaching him several traditional and old-time songs. While he was selling trees locally, he met Sara Dougherty (1898–1979). The pair married on June 18, 1915, and settled in Maces Springs, Virginia, where he worked various jobs while the two of them sang at local parties, socials, and gatherings for the next eleven years.

Around 1926, A.P.'s sister-in-law Maybelle Addington (1909–1978) began singing and playing guitar with Sara and A.P. and the trio started performing more regularly. In 1927, the group auditioned for Ralph Peer, a New York–based A&R man for Victor Records who was scouting for local talent in Bristol, Tennessee. The Carters recorded six tracks, including "The Wandering Boy" and "Single Girl, Married Girl," which began a relationship between the Carters and Victor that lasted until December 1934 and included such well-known songs as "Wildwood Flower" and "Keep on the Sunny Side."

By the decade's close, the group had become a well-known national act, but the Depression cut back their income considerably; by mid-1930 A.P. moved to Detroit temporarily while Maybelle and her husband relocated to Washington, D.C. In addition, A.P. and Sara's marriage began to fall apart, and the couple separated in 1932. By 1935, the group began short stints with ARC and then Decca. By 1937, they signed a lucrative radio contract with Mexican station XERF across from Del Rio, Texas. This led to contracts at a few other ultra-high power stations along the Mexican and Texas border that could be heard throughout the nation and into Canada.

Just as their career rebounded, Sara and A.P.'s marriage totally deteriorated and the couple divorced in 1939. Nevertheless, the group continued to perform, remaining in Texas until 1941, when they moved to WBT-AM in Charlotte, North Carolina. During the early 1940s the band briefly recorded for Columbia before they re-signed with Victor in 1941. Two years later, Sara decided to retire and move out to

California with her new husband, Coy Bayes (A.P.'s cousin), while A.P. moved back to Maces Springs, Virginia, and ran a country store. Maybelle Carter began recording and touring with her daughters, Helen, June, and Anita.

A.P. and Sara re-formed The Carter Family with their grown children in 1952, performing a successful concert in Maces Spring and quickly signed with the Kentucky-based Acme for whom they recorded nearly 100 songs. In 1956, The Carter Family disbanded for the second time. Four years later, A.P. died at his Maces Spring home. Following his death, The Carter Family's original recordings began to be reissued and have remained in print ever since. In 1966, Maybelle persuaded Sara to reunite to play a number of folk festivals and record an album for Columbia. The Carter Family became the first group to be elected into the Country Music Hall of Fame in 1970. Starting in the late 1950s, June Carter—who married Johnny Cash in 1968 and who died in 2003—enjoyed a solo career as a country singer. June's stepdaughter, Rosanne Cash, has enjoyed great commercial success beginning in the early 1980s.

Clifton Chenier (1925–1987): By mixing Cajun two-steps and waltzes with blues, R&B and rock 'n' roll, Chenier not only created the infectious sound of modern zydeco but earned the title "King of Zydeco." Chenier was famous for his outrageous outfits, consisting of capes and crowns (and a natty gold tooth), but it was his music that made him a legendary figure. From the early 1950s until he and his son C.J. took over the Red Hot Louisiana Band shortly before his death, Chenier brought this infectious, highly danceable music to audiences around the world.

Born on June 25, 1925, in Opelousas, Louisiana, to sharecropper parents, Chenier's father taught him to play the accordion. When he was twenty-two he moved to Lake Charles (where his brother, Cleveland, already resided) to work in the oil fields. He and his rub-board-playing brother made extra money playing La-La music at bars, weddings, and country picnics throughout the Texas-Louisiana bayous. The Chenier brothers were influenced not only by their creolized Cajun counterparts but also by the modern R&B sounds of Professor Longhair, Fats Domino, and Johnny Otis.

In 1954, Chenier signed with Elko Records, releasing "Cliston (*sic*) Blues/Louisiana Stomp," which sold well regionally. A year later he gained national attention when Specialty Records released "Ay-Tete-Fille (Hey Little Girl)." In 1956 Chenier finally quit his day job and hit the road with his band, the Zodico Ramblers. At various times such highly respected blues guitarists as Lonnie Brooks, Phillip Walker, and Lonesome Sundown were members of his band. Between 1957 and 1960 Chenier recorded thirteen more singles, but none of them scored a success on the charts.

Chris Strachwitz introduced Chenier to an entirely different and more diverse audience when he signed the musician to his Arhoolie Records label in 1964. Chenier's first album, *Louisiana Blues and Zydeco*, focused more on his Zydeco roots and produced a regional hit single. Then in 1966 Chenier appeared at the Berkeley Blues Festival in Berkeley, California, which exposed him to a wider audience and helped prepare a national audience for more of this regional sound.

For the next twenty years Chenier was a road man, touring across North America and Europe, becoming the unofficial ambassador for zydeco music, and recording albums regularly (including *I'm Here!*—a 1982 Grammy winner). Due to a problem with diabetes, Chenier severely cut back his touring schedule in the late 1970s. He toured and recorded as his health permitted, but he grew gradually weaker until he died from kidney failure.

Elizabeth (Libba) Cotten (1895–1987): A true African American songster who began playing music before the blues was established as a genre, Cotten's musical career began at about the age of eight when she started playing her older brother's banjo, and soon thereafter she learned to play the guitar. Cotten began playing the country dance tunes and ragtime songs that were so important in her native Chapel Hill, North Carolina, around the turn of the century. When she was twelve she heard a train in the distance, which inspired her signature piece "Freight Train."

In February 1910, she married Frank Cotten and did domestic work around Chapel Hill. The couple had a daughter, Lillie, and they soon became involved with the Baptist church. Cotten was too busy to play guitar very much, but she never laid it aside permanently. Like so many African Americans the Cottens joined the Great Migration, living briefly in New York City before settling in Washington, D.C., around 1940.

In the late 1940s, Cotten happened to begin working for the Seeger family, which eventually brought her back into the world of music. She first picked up young Peggy's guitar and started to remember the older songs from the turn of the century. Late 1957 to early 1958, Mike Seeger began recording Cotten, and within a year Folkways issued *Folksongs and Instrumentals with Guitar*. This was the dawn of the folk revival, and she was soon beginning to play for a new audience, starting with a joint concert with Mike Seeger at Swarthmore College.

In the next decade Cotten's graceful voice and delicate guitar and banjo picking was heard at folk festivals from New York to Los Angeles and on a series of recordings for Folkways. Her compatriots at this time included The New Lost City Ramblers, John Hurt, and John Jackson, as well as bluesmen like John Lee Hooker and Muddy Waters. During the 1980s, she continued to perform, received the National Endowment for the Arts National Heritage Fellowship, a Grammy, and recorded several albums before her advancing age forced her to stop performing.

Blind Gary Davis (1896–1972): One of eight children, Davis was raised by his grandmother on a farm just outside of Greenville, South Carolina, near his Laurens County birthplace. Davis began playing guitar at the age of six and singing at the Center Raven Baptist Church in Gray Court, South Carolina, around 1908. Around 1912, he was playing in a small string band in Greenville. About 1930 Davis moved to Durham, North Carolina, where he met Blind Boy Fuller, another of many blind street musicians of the time.

Within two years he relocated about 100 miles east to Washington, North Carolina, and was ordained as a Free Baptist Connection Church minister. Two years later the Reverend Davis and Blind Boy Fuller traveled to New York City to record for the American Record Company. Although Fuller and another blues singer, Bull City Red, recorded several blues selections, Davis remained true to his religious beliefs by focusing on gospel material such as "I Saw the Light" and "I Am the Light of the World."

In 1937, Davis and his second wife, Annie, moved to Mamaroneck, New York. The Reverend Davis often traveled to New York City for musical activities, which included not only performing on the streets and at churches but eventually recording for Continental, Folkways, and Prestige. Three years later the Davises moved to 169th Street in Harlem, where they remained until 1958. Davis then became a minister at New York's Missionary Baptist Connection Church and also began teaching guitar to an increasingly diverse group of aspiring musicians, such as folk-based guitarists Jerry Garcia, Ry Cooder, Bob Dylan, and David Bromberg. These musicians in turn interpreted his songs, such as "Baby, Can I Follow You Down" and "Candy Man" to audiences across the world. Davis remained an active teacher, performer, and recording artist until May 5, 1972, when he suffered a massive heart attack on his way to a performance.

Reverend Thomas A. Dorsey (1899–1993): The acknowledged father of gospel music, Dorsey remains arguably the most influential figure ever to impact the genre. Dorsey penned many of the best-known songs in the gospel canon, among them "Take My Hand, Precious Lord" and "Peace in the Valley"; founded the National Convention of Gospel Choirs and Choruses; and pioneered the richly talented Chicago gospel community in the 1930s, which included Mahalia Jackson and Sallie Martin.

Dorsey was born in Villa Rica, Georgia, on July 1, 1899, and raised in the Atlanta area all the while learning to play the piano and absorbing older hymns, blues, and jazz. Dorsey moved to Chicago in 1918 and during the 1920s (as "Georgia Tom") he became a prolific composer, authoring witty, slightly racy blues songs like "It's Tight Like That" as well as playing piano for various acts, including legendary vaudeville blues singer Gertrude "Ma" Rainey.

As early as 1921, he wrote the gospel song "If I Don't Get There," which gained him a small local reputation and left him uneasy playing only secular music. By 1932 he devoted himself to gospel music, organizing one of the first gospel choirs at Chicago's Pilgrim Baptist Church (which included future gospel star Roberta Martin) and founding the first publishing house devoted exclusively to selling music by black gospel composers. Shortly thereafter his wife and son died during childbirth, inspiring him to write "Precious Lord, Take My Hand" and settling his resolve to work exclusively with Christian music.

In 1933, Dorsey and another Chicago-based gospel singer, Sallie Martin helped found the annual National Convention of Gospel Choirs and Choruses, which introduced new songs to choir directors from across the nation. By now, Dorsey's songs were enormously popular, not only among black churchgoers but also among white southerners; by 1939, even the leading white gospel publishers were anthologizing his music. For the rest of his long career Dorsey devoted himself to composing, performing, and furthering gospel music. He worked especially closely with Mahalia Jackson in the 1940s and went into semiretirement in the 1960s but remained active until his death.

Bob Dylan (b. 1941): Born Robert Allen Zimmerman on May 24, 1941, in Duluth, Minnesota, Dylan grew up in the small town of Hibbing, Minnesota. In 1959, he entered the University of Minnesota, but he spent more time playing folk music in local coffee houses than studying. After his freshman year Dylan dropped out and hitchhiked to New York City, almost immediately locating and visiting his idol, Woody Guthrie. Having already adopted his Bob Dylan moniker (inspired by poet Dylan Thomas) the budding singer-songwriter became a staple on the Greenwich Village coffee house scene. By December 1961, Dylan had his first record contract with Columbia.

Dylan's debut album, *Bob Dylan*, was released in early 1962 and contained mostly covers of traditional material. His second release, 1963's *Freewheelin' Bob Dylan*, which contained many original protest tunes such as "Blowin' in the Wind," established Dylan as a political figure as well as a nationally recognized folk-based musician and songwriter. Throughout the rest of the 1960s, in albums such as *The Times They Are a-Changin', Another Side of Bob Dylan, Highway 61 Revisited, Blonde on Blond,* and the platinum-selling *Bring It All Back Home,* Dylan displayed a mixture of original material (much of it with social or political content) and folk songs with touches of rock and country thrown in. After a spring U.K. tour recorded in the documentary film *Don't Look Back,* Dylan stunned the music world during the summer of 1965 when his electric set at the Newport Folk Festival caused die-hard folk fans to accuse him of selling out to rock.

With Top-10 hits like "Rainy Day Women No. 12 & 35" and "Positively 4th Street," the sprawling album was a commercial as well as an artistic success with strong ties to the world of rock and pop music. In July 1966, he was badly injured in an upstate New York motorcycle accident and was forced to spend nearly two years in recuperation during which he spent months with both his family and his backup group The Band. Drawing on his interest in country music, Dylan's 1969 *Nashville Skyline* was not only recorded in Nashville with country session musicians but also featured a duet with Johnny Cash. His follow-up albums 1970's *Self Portrait* (a double album) and *New Morning* were not as well-received, and Dylan once more retreated into seclusion.

Dylan remained busy throughout the 1970s. In 1971, Dylan published a novel, *Tarantula,* and appeared at the Concert for Bangladesh, considered the model for all future benefit concerts. Shortly thereafter he headlined the hugely successful Rolling Thunder tour featuring Joan Baez, Joni Mitchell, Arlo Guthrie, and Allen Ginsberg, among others. The tour coincided with a new studio album called *Desire,* which quickly reached number one. In 1978, Dylan announced his conversion to Christianity, a move that informed 1979's *Slow Train Coming*, a number three hit that sold over a million copies.

Three years later, Dylan re-embraced Judaism via the Lubavitch Chabad movement, publicly marking his spiritual rebirth with a pilgrimage to Israel. In 1983, *Infidels* once more looked toward secular material, thus reassuring many of his longtime fans. Throughout much of the 1980s Dylan was a road man, touring with the likes of Tom Petty and The Heartbreakers and The Grateful Dead. In 1988 Dylan joined The Traveling Wilburys, an eclectic supergroup composed of Petty, George Harrison, Roy Orbison, and ex-ELO member Jeff Lynne, and they recorded two albums.

More recently Dylan has continued to tour regularly, working on his painting in his spare time. *Good As I Been To You* (1992) and *World Gone Wrong* (1993) marked a return to folk-based music. *Time Out of Mind* (1997), interestingly, won Grammy Awards in the Best Contemporary Folk Album, Album of the Year, and Best Male Rock Vocal Performance categories! In 2000, Dylan's song "Things Have Changed" on the soundtrack for the film *Wonder Boys,* added both a Golden Globe and a 2001 Oscar for Best Original Song to his string of major awards.

Life magazine named Dylan as one of the 100 most important Americans of the twentieth century, underscoring the fact that the folk-based singer-songwriter helped revolutionize popular music and bring a renewed sense of progressive social consciousness in American culture.

Fairfield Four (formed 1921): A gospel a cappella group of young men was organized in a Sunday school class at the Fairfield Baptist Church in Nashville at the beginning of the jazz age.

The Fairfield Four, as they soon became known, performed locally until the late 1930s when they made their first radio broadcast on WSIX. The first recording of the group came in 1941, when they were recorded by John Work for the Library of Congress. These recordings included "Don't Let Nobody Turn You Around," which became their signature number. The next year, The Fairfield Four won a promotional contest, resulting in a spot on high-powered WLAC, CBS radio's Nashville affiliate. This appearance resulted in a five-year association with WLAC, during which they became known as The South's Famous Fairfield Four. During this period, they toured extensively before a 1946 disagreement temporarily broke up the group.

Several years later, group leader Sam McCrary began to recruit singers outside Nashville, including James Hill from Alabama, "Preacher" Jones, and Isaac "Dickie" Freeman. Dickie's formidable bass singing underpinned the group's harmony for many years and can be heard on many of their classic recordings for Dot. In the early 1950s, the group split again and Hill, Freeman, and Thomas formed The Skylarks, another exceptional gospel quartet. Nearly thirty years later as part of a 1980 Quartet Reunion program in Birmingham, Alabama, The Fairfield Four were invited to reinvent themselves and perform in public again. Since then the group has thrived, despite the declining health and advancing age of group members. In 1989, the group was awarded a National Heritage Fellowship by the National Endowment of the Arts. Three years later Warner Brothers released their first major label release, *Standing in the Safety Zone*, which was nominated for a Grammy. In 1996, the group recorded with Charlie Daniels, John Fogerty, Lee Roy Parnell (nominated for CMA's Vocal Event of the Year for "John the Revelator") and

Elvis Costello. The group has recently received even wider recognition following their appearance in the film *O Brother, Where Art Thou* and touring in some of the subsequent tours associated with the film.

Brownie Ford (1904–1996): Thomas "Brownie" Edison Ford was born in 1904 in the Indian Territory near current day Gum Springs, Oklahoma. He grew up in both Native American and white American worlds. His life consisted of ninety-two years of travel, rodeoing, cowboy work, and wild west shows across Texas, Louisiana, and Oklahoma during the decades that marked major changes in transportation (from mules to jet planes) and music. In many ways, he represents a collision between the old and new west, the results of which is an interesting musical hybrid.

Ford learned to play the guitar in his teens, a talent he pursued for the rest of his life. His repertoire is as eclectic and interesting as his colorful life. Over the years, he learned to recite long epic poems about cowboy life, older British ballads such as "Black Jack Davy" and "Barbara Allen," American ballads like "Knoxville," and good-time tunes like "Don't Let the Deal Go Down" and "Burn the Honky Tonk Down." Even into his eighties, Ford was a raconteur of the first order, telling a bawdy story one minute, relating a tale about 1930s wild west shows the next, and then singing a late-nineteenth-century gospel hymn. In 1987, Ford was awarded a National Heritage Award from the National Endowment for the Arts. He died in Herbert, Louisiana, on August 27, 1996.

Arlo Guthrie (b. 1947): Although Woody Guthrie was hospitalized with a progressive neurological disease (Huntington's chorea) through most of his son's childhood, Arlo followed his father's lead by writing songs that often mixed social messages with humor. Taking the work of Woody as well as Pete Seeger and Huddie Leadbetter as early inspirations, Arlo began playing guitar at the age of six and became a popular coffee house performer by the middle 1960s. Although he polished his skills as a singer, songwriter, and musician in folk clubs, Guthrie reached a wide audience with his 1967 ironic, anti-establishment comic monologue cum story-in-song, "Alice's Restaurant," about the singer's conflict with the police and the draft board.

The "Alice's Restaurant" album remains Guthrie's best-selling recording. During the next decade, he recorded a series of folk-based recordings and was properly linked with singer-songwriters such as Bonnie Raitt and John Prine. In 1972, he enjoyed a brief run on the Top 40 charts with a heartfelt version of Steve Goodman's "The City of New Orleans." Unlike his father, whose social commentary was often biting, Arlo developed the persona of a minstrel who enjoyed the humorous ironies in current events.

During the 1970s, Guthrie made a series of albums for Warner Brothers. In the early 1980s, Guthrie launched his own label, Rising Son, which has reissued his Warner albums as well as serving as an outlet for new material. He continues to tour regularly, lending his name to causes as wide-ranging as Catholicism and environmentalism. Some of his more recent, notable albums are *All Over the World* (1991), *Son of the Wind* (1992), and *Mystic Journey* (1996).

Woody Guthrie (1912–1967): A native of Okemah, Oklahoma, it became clear from an early age that Woodrow Wilson Guthrie was an unconventional, bright, and musically inclined boy. Unfortunately, Guthrie lived a rather tragic life, which began with the death of his older sister in a house fire and included the institutionalization of his mother, financial hardships, and his own slowly debilitating struggle with Huntington's choera. In 1931, Guthrie moved to the panhandle Texas town of Pampa, where he married Mary Jennings in 1933 and began playing guitar and singing more regularly. The Depression and the Great Dust Storm (which began in the plains in 1935) made life a hopeless situation. Guthrie walked, hitched rides, and rode freight trains, heading west along with the mass migration of dust bowl refugees, joining all of the unemployed men and women from the lower Midwest who became known as Okies.

Arriving in California in 1937, Guthrie's rambling lifestyle and the ill-feelings displayed by Californians helped cement his outsider status, which became interwoven with his political and social views and voiced in such songs as "I Ain't Got No Home," "Talking Dust Bowl Blues," "Tom Joad," and "Hard Travelin'." He was soon able to reach a wider audience through radio broadcasts over KFVD (Los Angeles) and XELO (a high power border station located in Mexico), which brought together Guthrie and his new singing partner Maxine Crissman ("Lefty Lou").

In 1939, Guthrie headed back east and ended up in New York City, where audiences embraced him for his down-home wisdom and musical acumen. Guthrie, along with kindred spirits such as Burl Ives, Will Geer, and Josh White, particularly appealed to leftist organizations, artists, writers, and musicians. One year later, folklorist Alan Lomax recorded some of Guthrie's memories, stories, and hard-hitting songs for the Library of Congress.

Most of Guthrie's energies were devoted to live performances, however. He teamed with his fellow travelers during this period, most notably with The Almanac Singers (whose member's included Pete Seeger). Because of Guthrie's constant traveling and performing during the 1940s his first marriage dissolved. But in 1946, he married Marjorie Mazia, which led to a very stable relationship that enabled him to complete his somewhat autobiographical novel, *Bound for Glory*. The Guthries had four children: Cathy, who died at age four in a tragic home accident, Arlo, Joady, and Nora.

During World War II, Guthrie served in both the merchant marine and the army; and throughout his military duty, as in civilian life, his seemingly inexhaustible need to write and draw continued unabated. Upon returning from the war, Guthrie and his family settled in Coney Island, New York, and he wrote *Songs to Grow On,* a highly praised and well-known collection of children's songs. Shortly after its publication, he began to display the first signs of Huntington's chorea. His behavior and emotional health began to deteriorate, becoming increasingly erratic. By 1954, Guthrie admitted himself into Greystone Hospital in New Jersey. He was in and out of hospitals for the rest of his life, growing increasingly enfeebled until his death on October 3, 1967.

Aunt Molly Jackson (1880–1960): Mary Magdalene Garland grew up in a coal-mining family that was active in unionizing the mines. Throughout her life she wrote approximately 100 songs about the lives and struggles of local coal miners and was referred to as "a female Lead Belly" by Woody Guthrie. Married at age fourteen to Jim Stewart, who died in a 1917 mining accident, she bore two children and was trained as a nurse and midwife in her native Clay County, Kentucky. She married another miner, Bill Jackson, and earned the nickname "pistol packin' mama," because of her outspoken nature. It was in the late 1910s and 1920s that she began to write songs, such as "Harlan County Blues" and "I Am a Union Woman" and became known as "Aunt Molly."

In 1931, she came to the attention of a delegation, which included Theodore Dreiser and John Dos Passos, that was visiting Harlan County in order to investigate social injustices. This group helped introduce her to an audience outside of Kentucky. Blacklisted by mine owners, Jackson took to the road, visiting thirty-eight states to champion miners' rights and helping raise tens of thousands of dollars for miners. She moved to New York City in 1936 and continued to work to increase the awareness of miners' working conditions. Between 1935 and 1939, she recorded more than 150 of her songs for the Library of Congress. She also appeared with Lead Belly, Josh White, and other activists as part of the traveling Cavalcade of American Song. She died in Sacramento, California, just as the folk revival kicked in and she was beginning to receive recognition from a new audience.

Mahalia Jackson (1911–1972): Jackson reigned as a pioneer and public interpreter of gospel music whose fervent contralto is recognized as one of the great voices of the last century. The influence of gospel on R&B and rock 'n' roll is now widely understood, and Little Richard has cited Jackson as "the true queen of spiritual singers." Jackson herself has often said that "rock and roll was stolen out of the sanctified church!" This is perhaps most clearly evident in the proto-gospel songs recorded in the 1930s through the 1950s by such singers as Jackson, Marion Williams, and Sister Rosetta Tharpe.

Jackson was born in New Orleans, and she was influenced by Bessie Smith and the rhythm and blues she heard all around her. She carried the rich musical heritage of her native city with her when she joined the Great Migration, moving to Chicago in 1927. Jackson initially earned her living as a domestic but soon found abundant work as a soloist at churches and funerals. She then joined The Prince Johnson singers, but emerged as a professional soloist in the mid-1930s first locally and then on tour with the Reverend Thomas A. Dorsey, as the two of them helped define modern gospel music. After World War II, she recorded first for Apollo (1946–1954) and then the more prominent Columbia Records, where she achieved broader recognition for songs such as "Move on Up a Little Higher" and "How I Got Over." She also lent her powerful voice and imprimatur to the civil rights struggles of the 1950s and 1960s, including a memorable appearance at the 1963 March on Washington. Jackson remained active as a singer and spokesperson for the movement until she died of heart failure outside Chicago in 1972.

Blind Lemon Jefferson (1893–1929): Jefferson became the first important country blues artist to record in the 1920s. He was the youngest of six children born to cotton farmer Alec Jefferson and his wife, Classie, who lived near Wortham, some sixty miles south of Dallas. It's assumed he had been born blind, but older musicians who knew Jefferson in the 1920s suggested he was not totally blind. In later life, he wore large wire glasses—not dark glasses—and his songs were full of strong visual images that suggested that he had some vision at one point in his life.

Long a musician, in 1925 Blind Lemon Jefferson began to win nationwide fame through his recordings. Most of these were done for Paramount, an interesting small record company that was a subsidiary of a chair company in Wisconsin. Dallas-based blues pianist Sam Price had put Jefferson in touch with the company. After a couple of lesser releases, the guitarist recorded two pieces—"Got the Blues" and "Long Lonesome Blues"—for a single 78 rpm in February 1926. The former showed off his unique guitar playing and high forceful voice. Once recorded, he exploded like a bombshell on the fledgling blues scene in 1926. Sales of over 100,000 were rumored, and the metal masters Paramount made had worn out in three months; Jefferson had to return to the studios to re-record his two-sided hit. Within a matter of months, he would travel north to Chicago to record every three or four months; the company eventually created a special label for him, one trimmed in bright lemon yellow.

Between 1926 and his untimely and mysterious death around December 1929, Jefferson recorded over 100 titles. Many of these records were not only best-sellers in their time (they were featured in big display ads in big northern newspapers like the *Chicago Defender*) but became blues standards, reissued and copied by later generations of blues musicians and folk singers. The best-known include "Matchbox Blues," "See That My Grave Is Kept Clean, "Easy Rider Blues," "Broke and Hungry," and "Jack O' Diamonds." Their success won him the title King of the Country Blues and opened the door for the commercialization of this music.

Flaco Jimenez (b. 1939): Born Leonardo Jiménez on March 11, 1939, in San Antonio, Texas, Flaco's grandfather Patricio learned his initial accordion skills from German neighbors in south Texas in the early twentieth century. Flaco's father, Don Santiago Jiménez Sr., continued this tradition around San Antonio and is widely recognized as the progenitor of modern conjunto accordion playing. Known as El Flaco, "the skinny one," Flaco played bajo sexto with his father and made his recording debut in 1955 on "Los Tecolotes." He soon switched over to accordion, recorded with the group Los Caminantes, and enjoyed regional success with topical songs like "El Pantalon Blue Jean" and "El Bingo."

Like other regional artists (like Clifton Chenier and Lightnin' Hopkins) who benefited from the folk boom, Jimenez's Arhoolie Record albums and singles attracted a following outside Texas. He eventually appeared on stage with Bob Dylan, and his 1973 appearances with the Texas-bred Doug Sahm and Band brought him to the attention of rock fans. The eclectic Ry Cooder began using him on records as well as on his infrequent tours. *Tex-Mex Breakdown,* in particular, displayed Jiménez's roots while expanding his musical horizons. Jimenez has won multiple Grammys, has worked with Peter Rowan and the Free Mexican Airforce, and toured the United States and Europe as a solo act.

Robert Johnson (1911–1938): Johnson was born on May 8, 1911, to Julia Major Dodds and Noah Johnson in Hazelhurst, Mississippi. Until his late adolescence, his name was Robert Spencer after his stepfather changed his name from Dodds to Spencer when he ran from Mississippi after some personal problems. Johnson reclaimed the name of his natural father when he was about sixteen.

Music attracted Johnson as a child—his first instruments were the Jew's harp and the harmonica. In his early teens, he started playing guitar. Around June 1930, he met an older blues musician, Son House, whose music deeply affected him. Unwilling to be part of the sharecroppers' backbreaking work, Johnson moved south to Hazelhurst, Mississippi, where he played at local juke joints and lumber camps and met an older woman named Calletta "Callie" Craft. The couple was married in May 1931, but the marriage was kept secret.

The year and a half he spent in southern Mississippi was critical in Johnson's musical development. When Johnson returned to Robinsonville, Son House and fellow guitar wizard Willie Brown were astonished by his rapid progress as a Delta blues musician. Fueled by rumors that Johnson had traded his soul to the devil in exchange for his guitar expertise and clear talent, his career took off.

In live performances, Johnson played traditional material, some of his own songs, and even popular songs of the day. When he decided that he had progressed enough to make commercial phonograph records (1936), he approached H. C. Speirs, a white record store owner in Jackson, Mississippi, who had previously arranged sessions by bluesmen for Paramount Records. Speirs teamed him up with Ernie Oertle, an ARC (Columbia Records) scout. Johnson traveled to San Antonio late in November 1936, where he recorded such significant songs as "Kindhearted Woman Blues," "I Believe I'll Dust My Broom," "Sweet Home Chicago," "Rambling on My Mind," "When You Got a Good Friend," "Terraplane Blues," "32–20 Blues," "Cross Road Blues," and "Walking Blues" over a five-day period. Johnson returned to recording in June 1937, this time at a Dallas field session. At this, his final session, he recorded "Hellhound on My Trail," "Me and the Devil Blues," "Stop Breakin' down Blues," and "Love in Vain," among others.

Over the next year, Johnson traveled throughout the Delta and as far afield as St. Louis and Memphis. On August 13, 1938, at a juke joint named Three Forks, near Greenwood, Mississippi, Johnson played his last gig. Many rumors surrounded Johnson's death (including stabbing and poison), but his death certificate, which was finally located in 1968, merely verified his death. He was laid to rest at a small church in Morgan City, Mississippi, near Greenwood.

Around 1963, Columbia released the first long-play records of Johnson's 1936–1937 recordings. These records introduced Johnson's compelling music to a new (largely white) audience. In 1990, Columbia reissued Johnson's recordings in their Roots 'n' Blues series, a double compact disc set that has sold over one million units. Shortly thereafter Robert Johnson was featured on a U.S. Post Office stamp. Early in the twenty-first century, Johnson remains one of the most prominent and compelling of the early Delta blues musicians.

Kingston Trio (formed 1957): One of the most influential groups during the height of the folk revival, The Kingston Trio (Bob Shane, Nick Reynolds, and Dave Guard) was formed in San Francisco in 1957. The Kingston Trio had tremendous local success but became a nationally recognized group within eighteen months, following the unexpected success of the Civil War era murder ballad "Tom Dooley"—the number one selling single in 1958. Their charming harmonies and enthusiastic live performances endeared the trio to an America weary of fights between the new left and the hearings run by Senator McCarthy. A run of successful albums kept the group in the limelight well into the 1960s.

During the 1960s, however, the group's personnel changed several times, and The Kingston Trio's popularity waned in the face of these changes as well as the growing popularity of rock-based music. The arrival of The Beatles hurt The Kingston Trio, as well as other folk acts. Moreover, the success of more exciting and politically oriented folk-rock acts, such as The Byrds and Gram Parsons, rendered them increasingly old-fashioned and the trio was disbanded in 1968. In 1981, a Kingston Trio reunion was hosted by Tom Smothers on television. In 1987 the trio was on the road again, lead by original member Bob Shane, and they continue to perform and record.

Alison Krauss (b. 1971): Growing up in Champaign, Illinois, Krauss began learning to play the fiddle at the age of five. She entered her first fiddle contest at age eight, and four years later, she had become a student of bluegrass and the Illinois State fiddle champion. A talented fiddler, Krauss also possesses a clear bell-like voice, which is sometimes compared to Dolly Parton's.

At thirteen, Krauss began touring with her bluegrass band, Union Station, which recorded an album that caught the attention of Rounder Records president Ken Irwin, who signed Krauss the next year. Since then, she has turned out a steady steam of bluegrass and bluegrass-influenced albums for Rounder, including a video "I've Got That Old Feeling" that won CMT's Independent Video of the Year. Following Ricky Scaggs's lead, Krauss fought hard to bring bluegrass back into contemporary country music's mainstream with albums such as *I've Got That Old Feeling*, which won the 1990 Grammy for Best Bluegrass Recording. Three years later, she became the youngest woman to become a member of the Grand Ole Opry and soon thereafter began touring with popular country acts such as Alan Jackson, Amy Grant, and Garth Brooks. In 1995, she received five nominations at the annual Country Music Association awards. Krauss and Union Station's contribution to the soundtrack of the Coen Brothers' influential 2000 film, *O Brother, Where Art Thou?*, with Dan Tyminski providing the singing voice for George Clooney's character, stands as one of the film's musical highlights and helps solidify her bluegrass roots.

Lead Belly (1885–1949): Huddie Leadbetter grew up in the all-black world of Caddo Parish, Louisiana. Lead Belly's musical talents quickly blossomed, and he began to employ his talents at local sukey-jump parties and country dances. Around 1905, he left home to wander, making a living as an itinerant minstrel, a farm laborer, and cotton picker. During this time he married his first wife, Lethe, and roamed around Dallas (circa 1912) with the legendary blues singer Blind Lemon Jefferson.

In 1915, Lead Belly was jailed for assault, while living in Harrison County, Texas, and was sentenced to time on a local chain gang. He escaped within several months and decided to move on to De Kalb, in northeast Texas. One night during the winter of 1917, Lead Belly was accused and convicted (probably wrongly) of fatally shooting a local roustabout, Will Stafford; he was then sentenced to a long term of hard labor that landed him in Sugarland Prison. Lead Belly served seven years of a thirty-year sentence in Texas, performing hard labor before being granted a full pardon in 1925 by Patt Neff, then governor of Texas.

After receiving Neff's pardon, Lead Belly returned to Mooringsport, Louisiana, and for the next five years played music and worked farm labor jobs. But by 1930, he was in trouble for allegedly cutting a white man, which earned him six to ten years at the harsh Louisiana state prison farm at Angola. In 1933, distinguished Texan folklorist John Lomax ran into Lead Belly. Lomax recorded Lead Belly as part of his July 1933 recordings for the Library of Congress. Lead Belly hooked up with Lomax after his release in August 1934. Over the next year Lead Belly married Martha Promise, made a public splash in New York City, recorded for ARC, and became the subject of a book (*Negro Folk Songs as Sung by Leadbelly*).

During the 1940s Lead Belly eked out a living playing at folk clubs, left-wing organizing parties, and the occasional recording. He toured briefly in Europe, and it was in Paris in 1948 where he was diagnosed with Lou Gehrig's disease (amyotrophic lateral sclerosis). Some six months later, he succumbed to the disorder on December 6, 1949. Ironically, one year after his death "Goodnight Irene" (perhaps his best-known song and one that he had learned from his uncle Bob Ledbetter) became the nation's number one hit for The Weavers.

Uncle Dave Macon (1870–1952): Perhaps the oldest folk musician to record commercially, David Harrison "Uncle Dave" Macon provided the direct link between minstrelsy and modern country music. Macon's father (a Confederate captain in the Civil War) moved the family to Nashville from nearby Warren County and bought the city's Broadway Hotel, where his son learned songs and to play the banjo from the vaudeville artists who stayed there. He soon started the Macon Midway Mule and Wagon Transportation Company, which carried goods between Murfreesboro and Woodbury. Macon performed at venues along the route, paving the way for his career as a professional entertainer following the collapse of his business in 1920.

Two years later, at the age of fifty-two, Macon began his professional career. He became the first star of *The Grand Ole Opry* (before Nashville's WSM) when it was launched in 1925. In 1927, Macon formed The Fruit Jar Drinkers with Sam and Kirk McGee and Mazy Todd, who recorded some of the finest old-time string band recordings. Between 1924 and 1938, Macon recorded over 170 songs, which makes him one of the most recorded early country stars. Despite the fact that he was in his fifties and sixties, these raucous, engaging recordings, most notably the traditional songs "Arkansas Traveller," "Cindy," and "Soldier's Joy," remain timeless performances. Macon appeared with Roy Acuff in the 1939 film *Grand Ole Opry*, which displayed his abilities as showman. Macon finally stopped touring in 1950, making his last appearance at the Opry in March 1952. He was elected to the Country Music Hall of Fame in 1966.

Wade Mainer (b. 1907): Born into a musical family in the country near Weaverville, North Carolina, Mainer quickly became a fine singer and talented banjoist whose unusual two-fingered style set the stage for bluegrass picking. He played in small string bands in western North Carolina during the 1920s, including one lead by his older brother, J.E. In 1937, after an extended stint performing with J.E. Mainer's Mountaineers, Wade formed his own band, the Sons of the Mountaineers, which played throughout the Carolinas. Many of his friends from western North Carolina, including Wade Morris, Jay Hugh Hall, Steve Ledford, and Clyde Moody, performed in this proto-bluegrass band. He got the chance to record for Bluebird in the late 1930s and early 1940s; he's particularly remembered for his 1939 recording of "Sparkling Blue Eyes." Shortly after the close of World War II, he made some recordings for the Cincinnati-based King label. By the mid-1950s he'd relocated to Flint, Michigan, to work for Chevrolet. After retirement from the Chevrolet plant in the 1970s, he began playing more and returned to record for the local Old Homestead label. As of 2004, Mainer (often in the company of his wife, Julie) still plays banjo and sings and is often honored as one of the founders of bluegrass.

Lydia Mendoza (b. 1916): Born in Houston, Texas, Mendoza has been one of the most influential Mexican American (Tejano) musicians of the twentieth century. Raised in a large family in which home-grown music was a daily activity, Mendoza made her recording debut in a San Antonio hotel room—studio set up by OKeh Records to record La Familia Mendoza (a.k.a. Cuarteto Carta Blanca) in 1928. Early in her career, Mendoza recorded "Mal Hombre," which became her signature song and remains a classic on both sides of the border.

Her mother, Leonora Mendoza—a guitarist, vocalist, and the musical head of the family—taught the other family members to sing and play violin, mandolin, and percussion instruments. When not playing music, the family supported itself by working as migrant laborers. Manuel J. Cortez (owner of KCOR in San Antonio) was the first to manage Mendoza's career, giving her a weekly radio segment late in 1928. Their 1928 OKeh recordings brought the family a windfall of $140, enabling them to migrate to Detroit.

Returning to Texas in the early 1930s, the family survived by performing in San Antonio's Plaza de Zacate. This time they caught the attention of the Bluebird Record Company (a subsidiary of RCA Victor), which invited them to record in 1934. Their initial Bluebird session yielded six songs, including "Mal Hombre." The sales of these records encouraged Bluebird to call them back once or twice a year; between 1934 and 1940 Mendoza recorded just under 200 songs.

Leonora organized a family variety show with Lydia as the featured solo singer and guitarist as part of a family ensemble touring as Las Hermanas Mendoza. The Mendoza Family toured the Southwest as far as California and into the Midwest as far as Chicago until the early 1940s when the rationing of tires and gasoline brought about by World War II halted the family tours. The touring and recording resumed after the war until Leonora's death in 1952. Throughout the 1950s Lydia recorded for local labels such as Falcon and Ideal, along with a few sessions for Victor. It was during this time that she acquired the nickname "La Alondra de la Frontera" (the Lark of the Border). Also popular in Mexico, she often toured there and continued to live and perform on both sides of the border.

A new phase of her career began in 1971 when Mexico, not the United States, chose Mendoza to represent them in the Smithsonian Festival of American Folk Life. She appeared at the Library of Congress in 1977 at the request of the American Folk Life Center's Ethnic Recordings in America conference. These events began her wider general recognition, including a 1982 National Heritage Award from the National Endowment for the Arts. She continued to sing publicly until the mid-1980s when a stroke prevented her from playing the guitar with enough facility to appear in public. Mendoza remains the matriarch of Tejano music.

Bill Monroe (1911–1996): William Smith Monroe, the father of bluegrass, was born to father J. B. "Buck" and mother Malissa Vandiver on September 13, 1911, on a farm in Jerusalem Ridge, in western Kentucky just outside Rosine. His mother played accordion, fiddle, and harmonica, while his brothers and sisters played guitar and fiddle. By age eighteen, Monroe was already an accomplished musician, and in the summer of 1929, he joined his brothers, Birch and Charlie, to work at the Sinclair refinery in Whiting, Indiana, and perform music.

After nearly four years of struggling, the peripatetic Monroe Brothers (Bill and Charlie) eventually raked up radio appearances in Iowa, Nebraska, and the Carolinas. In 1936, the pair worked on the *Crazy Barn Dance* on Charlotte's WBT. That same year, they made the first of nearly sixty recordings for RCA's Bluebird label.

After a rough start in the Mid-South, Bill relocated to Atlanta and put together his first Blue Grass Boys band, including Cleo Davis (guitar and lead vocal), Art Wooten (fiddle),

Amos Garin (bass), and himself (mandolin). The band auditioned for *The Grand Ole Opry* on WSM in October 1939, beginning a relationship that lasted more than fifty years. Although its personnel changed much over the years, the classic line up was in place by the winter of 1945, when a young banjo player named Earl Scruggs and guitarist-vocalist Lester Flatt joined the band. Scruggs's three-finger banjo style, which he picked up in western North Carolina, became the standard for future bluegrass groups.

In 1951, Monroe bought some land at Bean Blossom in Brown County, Indiana, where he established a "country park" that became his second home. By the early 1960s, Monroe became involved in the folk revival, which earned him the "Father of Bluegrass" moniker. He participated in the First Annual Bluegrass Music Festival at Fincastle, Virginia, in 1965, followed two years later by his own Bean Blossom Bluegrass Festival. During the 1960s, there were many young musicians, including Bill Keith, Peter Rowan, Byron Berline, Roland White, and Del McCoury, whose careers included stints with Monroe.

In 1970, Monroe was elected to the Nashville Songwriters Association Hall of Fame and, more important, the Country Music Hall of Fame in Nashville. Monroe maintained a busy touring and recording schedule throughout the 1970s, but in 1981 he was diagnosed with cancer. This slowed him down, but he rarely stopped performing. In 1986, in celebration of his fiftieth year in the music business, Monroe took off on an exhausting fifty-state tour, traveling by car and bus as he had always done. In 1991, he was inducted into the International Bluegrass Music Hall of Honor; two years later he was awarded the Lifetime Achievement Award by the National Association of Recording Arts and Sciences. Monroe was presented with the National Medal of the Arts in 1995 by President Clinton.

Following a stroke in April 1996, Monroe was hospitalized in Baptist Hospital in Nashville and in Tennessee Christian Medical Center in nearby Madison. He passed away at Northcrest Home and Hospice in Springfield, Tennessee, on September 9, 1996, only four days before his eighty-fifth birthday. His funeral took place at the old Ryman Auditorium, where he had graced the stage of *The Grand Ole Opry* for decades.

New Lost City Ramblers (formed 1958): The influential old-time string band New Lost City Ramblers was founded by New York City natives Mike Seeger, John Cohen, and Tom Paley. Rather than merely mimicking the folk groups of the day, such as The Kingston Trio, these men preferred to look further back to some of the early recording artists like Uncle Dave Macon, Charlie Poole, Gid Tanner and the Skillet Lickers, and the Carolina Tar Heels. Mike Seeger also emphasized the importance of contemporary fieldwork by looking for old-time musicians, such as Doc Boggs, who had been either forgotten or overlooked by commercial record companies. Although their adherence to traditional values limited their commercial potential, this important group enjoyed the admiration of their peers and played a crucial role during the urban folk revival that blossomed in the early 1960s.

The original band remained intact until 1962, when Paley returned to his teaching career. Another New Yorker, Tracy Schwartz joined primarily as a fiddle player, but his addition also resulted in a broadening of the Ramblers' repertoire. They began to incorporate more unaccompanied ballads as well as traditional bluegrass music into their programs and recordings, which did not diminish the trio's base of support on the college and coffee house circuit. After ten years, the group decided to take up more individual projects, though they never formally dissolved. Cohen pursued his interest in photography, producing several excellent documentary films and taught for many years at the State University of New York at Purchase. Schwartz and Seeger, meanwhile, performed with different musicians, and together formed the short-lived Strange Creek Singers in the 1970s. Cohen, Seeger, and Schwartz reunited in 1997 for *There Ain't No Way Out* and continue to perform on an ad-hoc basis, bringing their eclectic mix of American folk music to a twenty-first-century audience.

Gabby Pahinui (1921–1980): Referred to as "The Father of the Modern Slack Key Era," Philip Pahinui was the prime influence that kept slack key guitar from dying out in the Hawaiian Islands. The modern slack key era (characterized by his interpretation of Hawaiian traditional tunes, popular standards, and original pieces performed with virtuosity and as a solo instrument) began shortly after World War II when Pahinui made his first recording. His five earliest recordings from the 1940s (78 rpms on Bell and Aloha Records) are especially impressive, inspiring and astonishing his peers. Pahinui's status as a musician was enhanced by his expressive vocals and soulful falsetto, which inspired many local singers. The Gabby Pahinui Hawaiian Band of the 1970s remains the quintessence of the complexities offered by the use of multiple guitars. In addition to its leader, the band featured two other virtuoso slack key guitarists, Leland "Atta" Isaacs Sr. and Sonny Chillingworth, along with Pahinui's sons, Cyril and Bla Pahinui.

Peter, Paul, and Mary (formed 1961): Blending original material with folk-based songs, Peter, Paul, and Mary was the most popular singing group in the United States just before the Beatles arrived. More than forty years later, despite several sabbaticals, they are still performing and recording together regularly. The group, assembled by musical entrepreneur Albert Grossman, brought together singer-songwriter Peter Yarrow, former Broadway singer and Song Swappers member Mary Travers, and singer-comedian Noel "Paul" Stookey to capitalize on the folk boom. The group, however, immediately harked back to the early 1950s heyday of The Weavers, especially Travers, who reminded many of Ronnie Gilbert, and the left-wing political commitment both groups shared and that the trio maintains today.

Signed to Warner Brothers Records in 1962, they released their debut album, *Peter, Paul & Mary*, which not only sold two million copies and won two Grammys but spun-off two popular singles: "Lemon Tree" and The Weavers' song "If I Had a Hammer." The next year, the group scored another enormous hit, "Puff, the Magic Dragon," co-authored by Yarrow, which is now a popular children's standard. The group's next single, released in June 1963, was "Blowin' in the Wind," written by the then little known folk-based singer Bob Dylan. They also appeared at the famous 1963 March on Washington. Over the next five years, the trio scored several more Top-40 hits, won another Grammy, and sold millions of albums. They also remained one of the most socially conscious folk-based groups, appearing at sit-ins and protest rallies.

In 1970, Peter, Paul, and Mary went on an extended sabbatical. Yarrow concentrated on political activism and produced three Puff the Magic Dragon animated TV specials, Stooky recorded eight solo albums, and Travers recorded five albums and starred in a BBC TV series. Eight years later, the trio reunited for an antinuclear benefit organized by Yarrow,

recording a live album called *Reunion*. In 1980, the group re-
formed and began touring frequently and recording. Peter,
Paul, and Mary remain as politically active as ever, supporting
peace in Central America and the Mideast, arguing against
nuclear power plants, and drawing attention to the plight of
the homeless and protesting Apartheid in South Africa. The
trio, which is still together, has appeared in several incredibly
popular specials for public television, and is recording albums
that continue to win awards.

Ola Belle Reed (1915-2002): Reed learned the claw-hammer
style of banjo playing as a child and grew up singing old-time
and gospel songs in her native western North Carolina. She performed with the North Carolina Ridge Runners in the 1930s
and after World War II, with her band the New River Boys
and Girls. During the Depression, like so many others from
the Southeastern states, she moved to Baltimore (with her
brother Alex), and started performing on radio stations across
the state and as far north as Wilmington, Delaware. In 1954,
together with her husband, Bud, she founded the popular
music venue The New River Ranch. She often appeared with
her husband and son David, with whom she established the
New River Ranch country park near Oxford, Pennsylvania.
This venue attracted a great many fans of her music from as
far away as southern New England. In the late 1970s, she
recorded an album that ensured she would be rightly remembered, although she perhaps tempted fate somewhat prema-
turely by calling it *My Epitaph*. She was the recipient of the
National Endowment for the Arts National Heritage Award
in 1986.

Almeda Riddle (1898-1986): "Granny" Riddle, a native of Greers
Ferry, Arkansas, grew up in a musical family; her father was a

fiddler, a singer, and a teacher of shaped-note singing. The church she attended throughout her life emphasized unaccompanied singing, a practice that reinforced her love of traditional unaccompanied ballad singing. In the mid-1950s, Riddle was "discovered" by John Quincy Wolfe, a professor at Arkansas (now Lyon) College who brought her to the attention of Alan Lomax. Lomax was one of several people who recorded her a cappella ballads, sacred songs, and lyric songs during the late 1959s into the 1960s. Riddles also traveled as far as New England to sing at places as diverse as Harvard and the Newport Folk Festival. When she died in 1986, three years after being awarded a National Heritage Award, Riddles left behind an extensive corpus of recorded traditional material songs that range from the gospel song "No Telephone in Heaven" to the British ballad, "The House Carpenter."

Jean Ritchie (b. 1922): A native of Viper, Kentucky, Ritchie was the youngest of fourteen children from a well-known family of traditional singers whose local reputation attracted the attention of English folk song collector Cecil Sharp. Sharp collected ballads from them in 1917 during one of his song-collecting expeditions to the Appalachian Mountains. Ritchie became immersed in the family traditions, including learning to play the mountain dulcimer from her father. Ritchie graduated with a bachelor's degree in social work from the University of Kentucky in 1946 and moved to New York City. She was first recorded in 1948 when arranger and Columbia A & R man, Mitch Miller, heard her demonstrating a dulcimer in a store. Miller was impressed enough to produce her debut, *Round and Roundelays*. She was soon introduced to Alan Lomax, who recorded her songs, both for his own collection and for the Library of Congress's Folksong Archives.

In 1952, Ritchie made her first trip to the United Kingdom under the auspices of a Fulbright scholarship, which afforded her the opportunity to trace the origins of her family's songs. While overseas, she appeared at the Royal Albert Hall and Cecil Sharp House, the headquarters of the English Folk Dance and Song Society. *Singing the Traditional Songs of Her Kentucky Mountain Family* was not only her first album but the first folk recording to be issued on the Elektra Records label.

Over the following decades she made innumerable television and radio appearances, performed across the United States, and recorded a wealth of traditional and self-composed material. She thrived during the height of the folk revival, and many folk song collectors have sought the Ritchie family as a source of traditional material. Her own composition "My Dear Companion" was recorded by Linda Ronstadt, Emmylou Harris, and Dolly Parton on their 1987 release *Trio*. A longtime resident of Port Washington, New York, Ritchie remains an active performer and was awarded a National Heritage Fellowship from the National Endowment for the Arts in 2002.

Jimmie Rodgers (1897–1933): Rodgers was the youngest son of a railroad man and a frail mother who died during childbirth when Jimmie was five years old. Following his mother's death, Rodgers was brought up in a series of foster homes in his native Meridian, Mississippi, occasionally accompanying his father on railroad runs. He showed an early interest in music and entertainment, and by his early teens Rodgers had learned black-face comedy routines and various singing styles as well as how to play several stringed instruments. Nonetheless, the railroad held a strong fascination for Rodgers, and he spent hours around the rail yards, where he picked up songs from the hoboes, switchers, and crewmen.

In 1920, Rodgers married and soon had a baby daughter. His wife and daughter stayed with him through the often lean and difficult twelve years that followed, during which he threw together pick-up bands and toured with traveling tent shows when he was not working on the railroad. Four years after his marriage, Rodgers was diagnosed with tuberculosis, which was then incurable. He was hospitalized and very nearly died. On the doctor's recommendation, Rodgers and his family relocated for the clean air of Asheville in the mountains of western North Carolina. Before long, he appeared on WWNC, performing locally with the Tenneva Ramblers, a.k.a. The Jimmie Rodgers Entertainers.

This was the act that made its way across the mountains in a borrowed car to audition in Bristol, Tennessee, for the Victor Talking Machine Company in early August 1927. RCA Victor's principal A & R man, Ralph Peer, was in town looking for local talent. Eventually, The Carter Family, The Stoneman Family, and Rodgers all began their recording careers at this time. Although he came with a string band, Rodgers recorded two solo songs, "Sleep, Baby Sleep," and "The Soldier's Sweetheart," beginning a legacy of over 100 recordings. The striking combination of an easy yet intense voice and his relaxed guitar work, along with the yodeling, caught Ralph Peer's attention. Even though Rodgers's Bristol sessions did not yield any big hits, Peer was quick to arrange a follow-up session a few months later in Camden, New Jersey. Soon thereafter "T for Texas (Blue Yodel #1)," which drew heavily on down-home blues, became a national phenomenon. The lyrics about women and hard times made an obvious connection to the everyday lives of people across the United States.

By 1928, Rodgers had risen from obscurity to stardom. He continued to record traditional and sentimental songs along with his blues-influenced numbers. It turned out that his sister-in-law, Elsie McWilliams, had considerable skill as a songwriter, a talent that he did not hesitate to call on over the rest of his shortened career. Free to experiment in the studio and unfettered by a country music establishment, Rodgers recorded songs that he thought would appeal to a wide audience. He also recorded with a variety of instruments, such as mandolin, jug, steel guitar, ukulele, banjo, tuba, harmony whistling, and musical saw. Furthermore, he shared the studio with black jazz musicians Louis Armstrong and Earl "Fatha" Hines.

Between 1928 and 1933, Jimmie and his family lived a hectic and exhilarating lifestyle. But his problem with tuberculosis hung like a specter surrounding him. Although he grew weaker as the 1930s progressed, Rodgers continued to record and perform. But he finally died on May 26, 1933, while on a recording trip to New York City. He left behind a recorded legacy that remains in print today; scores of Rodgers imitators; and a new generation of country musicians, notably Gene Autry, Jimmie Davis, and Ernest Tubb, who built their careers on his music.

Pete Seeger (b. 1919): Along with Woody Guthrie, Seeger is one of the major figures in folk-based music. Seeger is intrinsically linked with the folk boom of the late 1950s and early 1960s and helped introduce various forms of folk music to a mass audience. Seeger's father, Julliard musicologist Charles Seeger, was one of the founders of ethnomusicology and focused on folk and non-Western music. Pete began playing banjo in his teens and attended private schools, including Harvard, where he majored in sociology. In 1938, he dropped out of Harvard to travel around the United States, ultimately meeting influential folk musicians as diverse as Lead Belly and Woody Guthrie. Upon returning to New York City in 1940, Seeger formed the politically progressive Almanac Singers, whose revolving cast members at times included Woody Guthrie, performing a mixture of protest songs, dance tunes, and ballads. The Almanac Singers often performed at union rallies, strikes, and protests, disbanding in the early 1940s when Seeger was drafted.

After serving in the Merchant Marine Corp for nearly three years, Seeger returned to New York City in 1948 where he formed The Weavers. The first successful folk group, The Weavers enjoyed mainstream success as performers, including 1950's "Goodnight Irene," which remained the country's number one seller for several months. During the McCarthy era, The Weavers were considered too radically left wing, and in the early 1950s their concerts were often boycotted. In 1955, however, The Weavers triumphed with a wildly popular Carnegie Hall engagement, which helped set the stage for the urban folk revival.

Seeger began his solo career in 1958, and quickly became known as a major figure in his own right. As the writer or popularizer of songs like "If I Had a Hammer" (a hit for Peter, Paul, and Mary), "Where Have All the Flowers Gone," "Turn, Turn, Turn" (popularized by The Byrds in 1965), and "We Shall Overcome," Seeger often lent his name to progressive causes such as civil rights rallies, college campuses, labor strikes, and antiwar protests. In 1961, Seeger signed a contract with Columbia Records, which gained him an even larger audience but raised the brows of younger radicals who accused him of selling out.

By the end of the 1960s, Seeger broadened his scope to include African music and Latin American folk songs among his interests. He authored instruction manuals for guitar and banjo as well as headlined many pro-environmental events that often drew attention to the pollution of the Hudson River (near his home just north of New York City). In the 1970s, he helped form Clearwater, an activist group that educates schoolchildren about water pollution. Today Seeger continues performing and remains involved in environmental and socially progressive issues.

Ralph Stanley (b. 1927): A native of Stratton, Virginia, Stanley is one of the patriarchs of bluegrass. He and his older brother, Carter, formed the seminal bluegrass ensemble The Stanley Brothers in 1946, and he has been a professional musician ever since. After local successes fueled by radio appearances over WCYB in Bristol, Virginia, which brought their music to a regional audience, The Stanley Brothers caught the attention of the local Rich-R-Tone Label for whom they initially recorded. But it was their recordings for Columbia Records from 1949 until 1952 that brought their groundbreaking bluegrass to a national audience.

Between 1946 and 1966, when Carter died, The Stanley Brothers and The Clinch Mountain Boys ranked among the most celebrated traditional bluegrass groups in the world, operating in the same sphere as Bill Monroe, Flatt and Scruggs, Jim and Jesse, and The Osborne Brothers. Over the years, Stanley's band has included such important figures as Ricky Scaggs, Keith Whitley, Larry Sparks, and Charlie Sizemore. After Carter's death, Ralph looked inward and began singing even more of the older gospel and ballads that he learned as a child. It's this aspect of his repertoire that has attracted more recent listeners to Ralph Stanley and The Clinch Mountain Boys.

While he has long been revered by bluegrass and folk afi-cionados, Stanley's solid career has blossomed since the release of the film *O, Brother Where Art Thou?* In 2002, he won Grammy awards for Best Country Male Vocalist Performance and Album of the Year. He is the central figure in the D. A. Pennebaker-Chris Hegedus documentary *Down from the Mountain* and was the closing act for the 2002 Down from the Mountain tour. He was also awarded one of the first National Heritage Awards from the National Endowment for the Arts.

Statesman Quartet (founded 1948): Hovie Lister was twenty years old when he started organizing The Statesmen Quartet, but his career in southern gospel started as a protégé of Dwight Block, who was the piano player for the original Stamps Quartet. Lister's career began as piano player for The LeFevres in 1940; two years later he was wowed away by The Homeland Quartet. After four years with The Homeland Quartet, Lister joined the groundbreaking southern gospel group, The Rangers Quartet, playing the ragtime-style piano that he had heard Dwight Brock perform in the late 1930s.

It was not until 1948 in Atlanta, Georgia, that Lister (who was working as a DJ at the Atlanta Radio Station WCON) decided to move out on his own and organized the first version of The Statesmen Quartet. Lister wanted a flashy, emotional group that in some ways mirrored the performance practices of African American gospel quartets, which he admired for both their musicianship and their ability to hold a crowd in their hands. This radical move was too much for some of the more conservative friends of southern gospel music, nonetheless the formula eventually proved successful.

The great early 1950s lineup of Statesmen, consisting of Lister, Jake Hess, Cat Freeman, and Big Jim "Chief"

Weatherington, not only soared artistically but also scored high marks with southern gospel fans. With some variations, this group was mostly intact for about twenty-five years and The Statesmen Quartet remained at the top ranks within their field. Today, along with The Blackwood Brothers and The Cathedrals, this group remains one of the top traditional-based southern gospel quartets.

Gid Tanner (1885-1962): It is difficult to separate the importance and recordings by Georgia fiddler and vocalist Tanner from his band mates, most notably The Skillet Lickers. The original members of the Lick the Skillet Band—Riley Puckett, Clayton McMichen, and Fate Norris—had been performing in various combinations around Atlanta since the early 1920s. In 1924, however, Tanner (a fiddle-playing chicken farmer from north Georgia) and the blind guitarist Puckett recorded together to become Columbia Records' first hillbilly talent.

Two years later, when McMichen and Norris were added to their basic duo, they first recorded as Gid Tanner and The Skillet Lickers. Over the years, there were many group variations; other significant members included Lowe Stokes (fiddle), Bert Layne (fiddle), Hoke Rice (guitar), Gid's brother Arthur (banjo, guitar), and Gid's teenage son Gordon (fiddle). By the end of their Columbia Recording career in 1931, they had cut eighty-eight selections, including fiddle tunes, traditional ballads, and pop songs, plus little comedy skits—most notably the multipart "A Corn Licker Still in Georgia." In 1934, Gid Tanner and The Skillet Lickers once again recorded for Bluebird and scored big with "Down Yonder," which sold nearly one million copies over the next fifteen years. After The Skillet Lickers dissolved in the late 1930s, Tanner continued to play the fiddle, but made his living as a chicken farmer until he died in 1962.

Dave Tarras (1897-1989): Tarras, a klezmer clarinetist of legendary talent who was schooled in classical music by his Ukrainian Jewish family, was born in Russia. His father was a wedding poet (badkhn) and trombonist, and his son followed his lead, starting with the flute when he was nine. Within four years Tarras switched to the clarinet, which he played until his death. By 1921, anti-Semitic laws, pogroms, and the Russian Revolution motivated Tarras to emigrate to New York City, following his older sister there.

Over the following decades, Tarras managed to become one of the best respected klezmer musicians in America. He played in bands like the Abe Schwartz Orchestra and performed with his own ensembles, playing for dances in Brooklyn, theatrical productions, radio commercials, and the Catskill Borsch Belt circuit in the summer. During the 1940s and 1950s, Tarras also lent his clarinet skills to jazz-oriented bands. His career underwent a renaissance and rediscovery in the 1980s as younger musicians discovered the musical cultural that Tarras, Naftule Brandwein, and Pete Sokolow, among others, developed in the years before rock 'n' roll. Shortly before his death, Tarass was awarded a National Heritage Award by the National Endowment for the Arts.

Uncle Tupelo (1987-1994): Uncle Tupelo was constructed around childhood friends and songwriters Jeff Tweedy and Jay Farrar, who grew up just outside of St. Louis. Originally drawn to punk, the duo soon turned their attention and talent to the folk-based and honky-tonk ballads of Gram Parsons and John Prine. They honed their unique blend of music for four years, recording two independently released albums before Sire/ Reprise Records brought their music to a wider audience in a 1992 album that was produced by Peter Buck of R.E.M. Lamentably, the band broke up in 1994 just as their bluegrass, old-time music, and pop was beginning to draw a larger, more diverse audience. Shortly thereafter Farrar went on to form Son Volt, and Tweedy formed Wilco, another influential group with roots-rock aspirations.

Muddy Waters (1915–1983): Waters defined the sound of Chicago blues and his early recordings (1948–1955) contain many gems. He directly influenced many rock stars from the 1960s, including the Rolling Stones who took their name from one of his best songs.

Born McKinley Morganfield near Rolling Forks, Mississippi, Muddy Waters is a nickname given to him in childhood. He was raised by a maternal grandmother in the small city of Clarksdale and was drawn to music at an early age. Influenced by legendary singers such as Son House and Robert Johnson, Waters soon mastered the bottleneck guitar style that was found throughout the Delta during the 1920s and 1930s. In 1941, a team of Library of Congress field collectors headed by Alan Lomax and John Work stumbled on Waters and returned to record him the following year. By this time he had several years of performing experience playing for dancers at juke joints and house parties.

Waters moved to Chicago in 1943 and, like so many others who left the Delta, never returned. Waters persevered with his music while working as a truck driver. For several years, he played at house parties on the south side and then at small bars. After the war ended and small independent record companies began looking for talent, Waters managed to persuade the operators of Aristocrat (which became Chess Records) to issue his first records. Propelled by the likes of Little Walter on harp, Otis Spann on piano, and Big Crawford on bass, these early recordings—most notably "Rollin' and Tumblin'," "Still a Fool," and "Standing around Crying"—show the transformation of traditional Delta blues into the keening, hypnotic, and driving Chicago blues.

Throughout the 1950s, Waters solidified and extended his early work success with a series of often brilliant recordings that were frequently emulated but rarely matched. These recordings remain the standards by which all other similar groups are measured. As the 1950s gave way to the 1960s, blues became less interesting to African Americans who started listening to soul and Motown. But the folk boom affected Waters when a younger white audience began to discover him in particular and blues in general. By the late 1960s, the demographics of his audience had changed from mostly black to mostly white, and Waters was being hailed as one of rock 'n' roll's preeminent forebearers.

Throughout the 1970s and until his death Waters continued to perform and record. Chess set up the *London Sessions* and the two-disc *Fathers and Sons* set, which paired Waters with younger white rockers. In 1977, his long association with Chess ended when Waters signed with Blue Sky Records, a Columbia-owned label operated by guitarist and singer Johnny Winter, who produced and appeared on four successful albums with his hero. Hobbled by the effects of a serious automobile accident and declining health, Waters continued to perform (often on crutches) before dying in his sleep at his Westmont, Illinois, home.

Doc Watson (b. 1923): Discovered in western North Carolina in 1960, Watson is a legendary performer who blends his Appalachian Scots-Irish musical roots with blues, country, gospel, and bluegrass to create his unique style. Blinded at infancy, Watson has spent his lifetime making music and is widely recognized for his wide and varied repertoire and as a most accomplished flat picker.

Watson was born Arthel L. Watson in Deep Gap, North Carolina, on March 23, 1923, into a family with a rich musical tradition. His mother, Annie Watson, sung many traditional secular as well as religious songs, and his father, General Watson, played the banjo. Doc's early instrumental experience was with harmonica and a homemade banjo, but at age thirteen he began his love affair with the guitar. Watson incorporated traditional songs (many coming directly from his family) as well as the popular material he learned from records and the radio. For decades, Watson played locally, often with his father-in-law, Gathier Carlton, a fine old-time fiddler.

When he was thirty years old Watson met Jack Williams, a local swing band piano player, and began to play rockabilly and country swing gigs for money. During the following years he toured eastern Tennessee and western North Carolina with Williams's band. But Watson never abandoned his roots, frequently getting together with his banjo-playing neighbor Clarence "Tom" Ashley. In 1960, Ralph Rinzler and Eugene Earle came south to record Tom Ashley and heard Watson's banjo picking; and they brought Watson and his music to a larger audience.

Since 1960, Watson has traveled and recorded extensively. He's made several dozen albums that usually feature his flat-picking guitar, many with his late guitar-playing son, Merle. Still active in the early twenty-first century, Watson remains an icon in American folk music, often representing Appalachian folk music at concerts and festivals across the world.

Whoopie John Whilfarht (1893–1961): Wilfahrt was born in 1893 on a farm near New Ulm, Minnesota, the grandson of immigrants from the Austria Black Forest near Switzerland. At age eleven he received a $1.50 accordion from his mother for Christmas and learned "Mariechen Waltz" (his theme song) while she hummed the tune as she did the housework. At age nineteen, he, his brother on clarinet, and a neighbor on trumpet formed a trio that performed for local weddings, dances, and socials. In 1914, Whilfarht moved from the farm to the town of New Ulm and got married.

Whilfarht soon formed a band of between ten and twelve pieces and widened his performance area in and around south-central Minnesota. In Swedish communities like Young America, the band played Swedish tunes; in New Ulm and Mankato it was German and Austrian; at Green Isle, Irish music was played; around Cumberland, Wisconsin, they played Italian music. In the mid-1920s, the band relocated to the Twin Cities and became regulars on several radio stations, most notably powerful WCCO. The band performed on Saturday nights at the American House in St. Paul for twenty-two years, which they augmented with other local gigs.

By 1930, the band had recorded on OKeh, Columbia, and Brunswick, usually as John (or Hans) Whilfarht's Concertina Orchestra. In 1934, the Kapp brothers, Dave and Jack, formed Decca and signed "Whoopee John." For the next fifteen years Whilfarht recorded dozens of selections for Decca, including the best-selling "Mariechen Waltz" and "Clarinet Polka." Throughout the course of his career, he recorded hundreds of 78 and 45 rpm records as well as long-play albums. In 1954 and 1955, his group was named the country's leading polka band by the National Ballroom Operators Association. Although he died of a heart attack at age sixty-eight, he remains a legend among polka aficionados in the upper Midwest.

Dewey Williams (1898–1997): A 1983 National Heritage Award winner, Williams served the African American shape-note singing community in southern Alabama for nearly ninety years. Williams was born in the Haw Ridge community in

Dale County in 1898 and sang and taught sacred harp since the early part of the twentieth century. His grandparents, who were slaves in Barbour County, also sang from the *Sacred Harp*, a songbook first published in 1844. The tradition, characteristically associated with white culture in the South, has enjoyed a vibrancy among African Americans in southeast Alabama for over a century. Along with the National Endowment of the Arts award, Williams's work was featured in Bill Moyers's PBS documentary *Amazing Grace*. The Dewey Williams Birthday Sing, which is still held annually in Ozark, Alabama, marks the beginning of the March through October singing season.

Bob Wills (1905–1975): James Robert Wills was born on a farm near Kosse, Limestone County, Texas. His father, known locally as "Uncle John," was a skilled fiddler and taught his son to play the mandolin so that he could accompany his father's playing. In 1913, the Wills family relocated to Memphis, Texas, with John and Bob playing for farm dances along the way to raise money for food. The family continued to play for local functions, but in 1924 Bob moved to Amarillo where he made enough money working on building sites and as a shoeshine boy to buy a fiddle. He then found work playing for dances on Saturday nights and made his first radio broadcasts over Amarillo's KGRS. By 1930, he was in Fort Worth, playing with guitarist Herman Arnspiger and Durwood Brown, along with vocalist Milton Brown as the Wills Band.

Later that year, Wills's band was sponsored on the 50,000-watt WBAP by the Aladdin Lamp Company, which was heard as far away as Oklahoma City. In 1932, Wills assembled a band that included his brother Johnnie Lee, and for the first time the band was known as The Playboys. Finally, in February 1934 Wills switched to powerhouse KVOO in Tulsa and finally got Bob Wills and The Texas Playboys on the airwaves.

In 1935, the group made their first historic studio recordings with a large band, consisting of twelve musicians. Wills remained in Tulsa, and during the late 1930s, he continued to shape and reshape his band, including electric guitarist Eldon Shamblin and several reed players, most notably Joe Ferguson. By 1940, his eighteen-piece band recorded his million-selling swing-style version of "New San Antonio Rose," the (Tommy Duncan) vocal version of his 1935 fiddle tune, previously known as "New Spanish Two Step." Although successful with his music, Wills's personal life was a mess—he was divorced and married four times between 1935 and 1941.

The year 1940 saw his feature film debut, when he appeared with Tex Ritter in *Take Me Back to Oklahoma*. Wills never cared for Hollywood, but he loved the cowboy image and traded on it for the rest of his life. During the 1940s, he scored country and pop chart hits with songs such as "Stars and Stripes at Iwo Jima." Due to unscrupulous advisers and accountants, he soon found himself heavily in debt, so he sold his Bob Wills Music Company and (accidentally with it) the ownership of "San Antonio Rose."

Throughout the 1950s, he recorded and toured extensively, and several times moved his base of operations. Wills continued to experiment, but the influence of television began to affect the dance halls; tastes had changed and he never recaptured the earlier successes. In 1962, he suffered the first in a series of heart attacks, but in 1963, he was back, even though he had sold the rights to use his name to Carl Johnson. Four years later and in increasingly ill health, Wills was elected to the Country Music Hall of Fame in 1968.

SIX

The Songs

American folk music is built on a foundation of songs. Literally thousands of songs, many of them quite familiar, come from traditional sources. These folk songs have been disseminated in many ways, including summer camp sing-a-longs, sound recordings, printed sources, peace rallies, and family gatherings. This chapter examines fifty American folk songs, which were selected based on their popularity, familiarity, durability, importance, or cultural and historical significance.

The songs come from many sources and many have enjoyed long lives. "River of Jordan," for example, has roots in pre–Civil War black musical culture, while "Barbara Allen" can be traced back to eighteenth-century England. "All My Trials," an anthem of the civil rights movement, comes to us from the Bahamas, where it was sung in the late nineteenth century. Others, such as "Peace in the Valley" and "Cool Water" were actually written and published in the 1930s, though they have often been passed along orally, and their underlying themes make them seem much older. Murders and tragedies are memorialized in songs such as "Frankie and Johnnie" and "Pretty Polly," both of which almost certainly go back to the Reconstruction era. Bigger-than-life figures, such as John Henry and Railroad Bill, are also celebrated in songs.

"Ain't No Grave Can Hold My Body Down":

> *Meet me Jesus, meet me.*
> *Meet me in the middle of the air.*
> *If these wings fail me, meet me with another pair.*
> *There ain't no grave gonna hold my body down.*
>
> *There ain't no grave gonna hold my body down.*
> *When you hear that trumpet sound.*
> *Gonna get up out of the ground.*
> *There ain't no grave gonna hold my body down.*

This powerful song about transformation and the Second Coming of Jesus has its roots in nineteenth-century spirituals and may have also been used as a work song. Its message and rich language appeals to black and white fundamental Christians who have been singing it for almost 100 years. It has been recorded by artists as diverse as black folk singer Odetta (1961) and a bluegrass band, the Caudill Family (circa 1950), but Bozie Sturdivant of the Silent Grove Baptist Church led an absolutely stunning version of this song as part of a church service documented by the Library of Congress in Mississippi in 1942.

"All My Trials": This song is believed to have Bahamian roots and is often cited as a Bahaman lullaby that was in oral tradition by the late nineteenth century. In the first half of the twentieth century, "All My Trials" was sung at black churches in the South; it came to greater public consciousness in the late 1950s and early 1960s as part of the folk revival through recordings by Bob Gibson (1959), The Kingston Trio (1959), and Joan Baez (1961), among many others. Its double message of a mother comforting her child on her deathbed along with the sense of struggle for justice also appealed to many who publicly protested during the civil rights era and against the war in Vietnam.

"Banks of the Ohio": Recorded as early as 1927 by Red Patterson's Piedmont Log Rollers, and subsequently by such early hillbilly artists as Ernest V. Stoneman, The Blue Sky Boys, and The Monroe Brothers (Bill and Charlie), this quintessential murder ballad about a man who kills his beloved because she would not marry him almost certainly dates back to the late nineteenth century. This lament about lost love, murder, and justice continued into the emerging bluegrass repertoire during the 1950s and 1960s. It was picked up by many folk-based singers such as Joan Baez, The Kossoy Sisters, and Jean Shilling, each of whom recorded versions of "Banks of the Ohio" in the early 1960s, perhaps as a presentiment of the emerging feminist movement.

"Barbara Allen": Of all of the ballads of British origins, "Barbara Allen" (or "Barbary Allen") is perhaps the most widely known in the United States. It was collected in America almost as soon as the first men and women from the United Kingdom migrated here and was included—as "Child #84"—in Harvard English professor Francis James Child's late-nineteenth-century collection of British ballads. Its simple and direct message of unrequited love clearly touches many people, for it has been collected across the entire country and has been recorded hundreds of times as early as 1927 by Vernon Dalhart. More recently, singers as far ranging as Hedy West (1967), Pete Seeger (1986), and cowboy singer Brownie Ford (1990) have recorded this timeless classic.

"Careless Love": "Can't you see, what careless love can do?" is a universal theme and the refrain for this song. "Careless Love" almost certainly emerged during Reconstruction, and its lyrics were first collected by folklorists in the early 1890s. This song's widespread appeal is underscored by the fact that both black and white folk singers recorded it. Early country music artists such as The Johnson Brothers (1927), Byrd Moore and His Hot Shots (1929), and Emry Arthur (1931) recorded their versions of this song, as did African American folk artists Lulu Jackson (1928) and The Four Southern Singers (1933). The tune has remained a staple in the repertoire of more contemporary folk singers like Dave Van Ronk (1959) and Mike Seeger (1973) as well as bluegrass bands like North Carolinians, Snuffy Jenkins, and Pappy Sherill and The Hired Hands.

"Casey Jones": Inspired by a true incident, "Casey Jones" is one of our most famous train wreck ballads. At approximately 4:00 A.M. on April 30, 1900, in the small town of Vaughn, Mississippi, at a long winding curve just above the town, train engineer John Luther "Casey" Jones noticed that a freight train was sitting motionless on the siding. But there were two separate sections of a very long train on the sidetrack this night; the rear one was a little too long to get all its length off the main track onto the siding. The freight train crews figured on "sawing by"; that is as soon as the passenger train passed the front part of the first train, it would move forward and the rear freight would move up, thus clearing the main track. But Casey's speed—about fifty-eight miles an hour—was more than the freight crews bargained for and #638 crashed into the freight train. Before the crash, Jones ordered the rest of the crew off the engine before his own futile solo attempt to avoid the wreck. "Casey Jones" was allegedly written by a Canton, Mississippi, African American railroad worker, Wallace Saunders, and published in 1909. The song was recorded by a variety of early traditional musicians, such as Furry Lewis (1928), Prince Albert Hunt's Texas Ramblers (1928), and Wilmer Watts and His Lonely Eagles (1929), and inspired Grateful Dead songwriter Robert Hunter to pen a popular song based on Jones's character.

"Cool Water" (Bob Nolan, 1940): This song is often labeled as a traditional western song. Certainly its themes are western enough (the absolute need for cool, cool water as one tramps across the range), but the song itself came from the fertile mind of Bob Nolan. Nolan, a member of The Sons of the Pioneers, also wrote "Tumbling Tumbleweeds" in 1932, when Leonard Sly (a.k.a. Roy Rogers) was a group member. "Cool Water" was first recorded by The Sons of the Pioneers in 1936 and sold well. It was a Top-10 hit for the group in both 1947 and 1948. Along with "Back in the Saddle Again," it is one of the best known of the folk-based western songs to come out of the 1930s.

"Corrina, Corrina": This turn-of-the-last-century lament about the faithless Corrina has inspired singers as different as The Westbrook Conservatory Entertainers (1929), Milton Brown and His Musical Brownies (1934), and Mississippi John Hurt (1966) to record the song. Sometimes known as "Alberta (Where You Been So Long)," it's been a favorite of both black and white folk singers for almost 100 years. Bob Dylan often sang it in the early 1960s and included it on his 1963 album *The Freewheelin' Bob Dylan*. The 1994 Hollywood film of the same title, which features Don Ameche, Whoopie Goldberg, and Ray Liotta, includes a nice version of the song performed by the iconoclastic folk-based singer-guitarist, Ted Hawkins.

"Crossroads Blues": Associated with Delta blues man Robert Johnson, "Crossroads Blues" remains one of the most chilling and compelling of blues performances. Hearing an early reissue of Johnson's recording from 1937 is one of the reasons why Eric Clapton became a blues guitarist in the early 1960s, and he continues to perform the song today. The song itself is about Robert Johnson's plea for help while standing at the crossroads of life. The song has been incorporated into the names of countless blues bands, and societies have been developed for the preservation and promotion of this music with music clubs and radio programs. In addition to Clapton's version, rock and pop artists as diverse as southern rockers Molly Hatchet and Steven Stills have covered this song since the early 1970s.

"Dark as a Dungeon" (Merle Travis, 1946): Protest and social commentary are two of American folk music's hallmarks, and this song about coal mining incorporates both. Written one evening and recorded the next day by Kentucky native Merle Travis, "Dark as a Dungeon" draws on his own family background. Travis's father and brothers were coal miners and his mother spent much of her time, as the song intimates, worrying about the dangers inherent in their trade. The song, which was covered by many singers such as Harry Belafonte (1962) and Joan Baez (1964), is in the tradition of other coal-mining songs written by Aunt Molly Jackson and Sarah Ogan Gunning.

"Frankie and Johnny": Elvis brought this story to a wide public in 1966 with the release of a splashy Hollywood film of the same name. The ballad itself, which is included in G. Malcolm Law's canon, can be traced back to St. Louis in the 1880s. It's the tale about an unfaithful man named Johnny and his girl Frankie. He steps out with Alice Fry or Nellie Blye (it depends on which version you like), and his general disrespect results in Frankie shooting Johnny because he "done her wrong." The song was in oral circulation for decades before the Winston-Salem, North Carolina–based medicine show singer Ernest Thompson first recorded it in 1924 under the title of "Frankie Baker." Subsequent versions of this popular two-timing ballad were recorded by Mississippi John Hurt (1928), Jimmie Rodgers (1929), Clayton McMichen (1937), The Kingston Trio (1961), and Doc Watson (1983).

"Freight Train" (Elizabeth Cotten, ca. 1904): Not the same song as "Freight Train Blues," which was recorded by Doc Watson, The Delmore Brothers, and others, this song clearly emanates from the creative mind and fingers of Elizabeth Cotten, an African American guitar picker from Chapel Hill, North Carolina. At the age of twelve—in approximately 1904—she composed "Freight Train" after hearing the distant moan of a train engine. But it went unrecorded for more than fifty years, until Cotten's music was first documented by Mike Seeger who convinced Moses Asch to release the material on his Folkways label. *Freight Train and Other North Carolina Folk Songs and Tunes* came out in 1958, and the title tune went on to become a standard tune in the repertoire of aspiring folk guitarists across the United States and in Europe. Since Cotten introduced the song, "Freight Train" has been recorded scores of times, including versions by Joan Baez (1961) and Norman Blake (1976).

"Froggie Went a-Courtin'": A children's ditty that remains in oral circulation across the United States, this song has been sung on playgrounds since at least the late nineteenth century. Its opening stanza is familiar to all:

> *Frog went a-courtin' and he did ride, Uh-huh,*
> *Frog went a-courtin' and he did ride, Uh-huh,*
> *Frog went a-courtin' and he did ride,*
> *With a sword and a pistol by his side, Uh-huh.*

The delightful story about the trials of romance still entrances children today, but it also appeals to adults who have recorded it (sometimes under alternative titles such as "Froggie Went a-Wooin'" or the "Frog and the Mouse") countless times since the 1920s. Among the best-known recordings are versions by Almeda Riddle (1959), John McCutcheon (1975), and Bob Dylan (1992).

"Goodnight, Irene": This song is most associated with Louisiana twelve-string songster Huddie Leadbetter, but it's clear that "Goodnight, Irene" existed before Lead Belly first recorded it for the Library of Congress in 1933. He was apparently singing the song, a tender waltz about a girl who is in love but is deemed too young to marry, as early as 1908–1909. It appears to date back to at least 1888 when the text of a song titled "Irene, Goodnight" surfaced in a souvenir songbook published by a traveling minstrel show called Haverly's American-European Mastodon Minstrels. How this song wandered into the repertoire of a black singer from the Ark-La-Tex region remains unknown, though Lead Belly certainly brought the song to a wide public. But it reached a huge audience in 1950 (the year after Lead Belly's death) when a version by The Weaver's reached number one on the pop music charts and stayed there for weeks.

"Grey Goose": "Go tell Aunt Rhodie that the old grey goose is dead" is both the refrain and the alternate title for this song. It's not only a popular children's play song but its simple melody can be found in dozens of piano instruction books and dulcimer primers. "The Old Grey Goose Is Dead" also found its way onto early hillbilly recordings by The Carolina Tar Heels (1929) and The Renfro Valley Boys (1932) in addition to the repertoire of Huddie Leadbetter (Lead Belly). Lead Belly probably did as much as anyone to keep the song in public consciousness by performing it at numerous concerts and recording it several times after he moved to New York City in 1935. It is Lead Belly's version that seems to have inspired artists like Pete Seeger (1963) and Richard Dyer-Bennett (1964) to include it on recordings aimed specifically at children.

"Hallelujah I'm a Bum": Despite the fact that Mac McClintock (a.k.a. Haywire Mac) copywrote and recorded this song in 1927, it has its roots in oral tradition. This old song was apparently first sung by railroad workers in Kansas in 1897 and by harvest hands who worked in the wheat fields of Pawnee County. It was subsequently picked up later by the International Workers of the World, who made verses of their own for it, and gave it a wide fame. McClintock's RCA Victor recording of "Hallelujah I'm a Bum" sold very well, further assisting in its dissemination. More recent recordings of this song include The New Christy Minstrels (1963) and U. Utah Phillips (1977).

> *Hallelujah, I'm a bum,*
> *Hallelujah, bum again,*
> *Hallelujah, give us a handout*
> *To revive us again. Oh, why don't you save all*
>   *the money you earn?*

If I didn't eat, I'd have money to burn.
Whenever I get all the money I earn,
The boss will be broke, and to work he must turn.

"Honey, Take a Whiff on Me": Although drug-infused songs garnered wide attention in the late 1960s, "Honey, Take a Whiff on Me" is one of the pioneering drug songs. Also known as "Cocaine Blues," this song made its recording debut in 1927 when Charlie Poole and The North Carolina Ramblers traveled to New York City to record for Columbia. The song puts down the use of alcohol and tobacco, while extolling the virtues of cocaine. Popular among both black and white recording artists in the late 1920s, the song seemed to drop out of favor for several decades before resurfacing in the late 1950s during the folk revival. Hoyt Axton (1963), Tom Rush (1972), and Eric Von Schmidt (1999) are among the musicians who have recorded the song more recently.

"House Carpenter": Along with "Barbara Allen," this is one of the most popular ballads of British origin ("Child #243") and also goes under the titles "The Deamon Lover" and "James Harris." It's a parable about inescapable punishment that follows a deep moral error about class, love, and marriage. This ballad has its roots in the same ancient myth that inspired Richard Wagner's operatic masterpiece, "The Flying Dutchman," in which a young woman sails endlessly with an other-worldly mariner until she shows remorse and breaks the magical spell. Mostly transmitted orally and through ballad books, the song was popular during the folk revival era. Traditional southern ballad singers such as Jean Ritchie (1961) and Almeda Riddle (1959) helped bring it to the attention of performers like Buffy St. Marie (1966). For inexplicable reasons, "House Carpenter" was widely collected by folklorists but only recorded a few times before the folk revival.

"I'll Fly Away" (Albert Brumley, 1929): Because it is so widely sung and known across the United States, the authorship of "I'll Fly Away" as a gospel song is often thought to be unknown. The prolific southern gospel composer Albert Brumley wrote the song in 1929, but waited three years to publish it as part of a songbook *Wonderful Message*. Before long, the song became widely popular across the South, and its composer was often overlooked. Its message is simple (with death comes freedom from the burdens of life and eternal rest in heaven) and has appealed to artists ranging from The Stanley Brothers (ca. 1954) to Caroline Hester (1961) with a very young Bob Dylan on harmonica to Albert Hash and The Whitetop Mountain Band (1979). It's also a staple of nearly every southern gospel quartet to perform since the middle 1930s.

"I'm a Man of Constant Sorrow": Known also as "I'm a Woman of Constant Sorrow," this lament has recently attracted a large new audience by way of The Coen Brothers' film *O Brother, Where Art Thou?* It appears in four guises in the movie, most movingly as a vocal performed by George Clooney (actually The Soggy Bottom Boys featuring Dan Tyminski's singing). The song itself was collected as early as 1913 and appeared in the repertoires of a small number of Kentucky ballad singers who were attracted to its lines about "seeing troubles all of my days." "Man of Constant Sorrow" received its recording debut in 1928 when Emry Arthur walked into a Chicago studio used by the Vocalion Company. A subsequent version by The Stanley Brothers (1950) kept the song in the repertoire of traditional bluegrass bands. Bob Dylan recorded it in 1962 on his self-titled first album, and Jerry Garcia of The Grateful Dead recorded the song on several occasions, though not for commercial release.

"In the Jailhouse Now": This song is about a good-time dandy, Ramblin' Bob, who liked to steal, gamble, play poker, and role dice—activities that eventually landed him in jail. Popularized by Jimmie Rodgers (1928), it's based on an older folk song that had previously been recorded by black musicians like Whistler's Jug Band (1924) and Blind Blake (1927). Like so many of Rodger's songs, "In the Jailhouse Now" spawned a host of imitations, including versions by Frankie Marvin (1928) and Bill Bruner (1930). The song has enough cache to be included on long-play records by Roy Bookbinder (1975) and Michael Cooney (1976) as well as appearing on the *O Brother, Where Art Thou?* soundtrack, performed by The Soggy Bottom Boys, featuring Tim Blake Nelson's singing. "In the Jailhouse Now," performed by Steve Earle and The V-Roys, is the lead track on the CD *The Songs of Jimmie Rodgers: A Tribute*, released on the Bob Dylan–run label, Egyptian Records.

"John Henry": Almost everyone has heard this song about the legendary steel-driving man, but few know that it has roots in a true story that probably occurred in West Virginia in the 1880s. The song, which was recorded as early as 1924 by Fiddlin' John Carson and has since been waxed hundreds of times by artists as diverse as Woody Guthrie, Burl Ives, and Odetta, relays the classic battle between man and machine. In this song, the steel-drivin' John Henry used a large hammer and stake to pound holes into rock, which were then filled with explosives that would blast a cavity deeper and deeper into the mountain. Eager to reduce costs and speed progress, some tunnel engineers used steam drills to power their way into the rock. According to some accounts, on hearing of the machine, John Henry challenged the steam drill to a contest. He won, but the superhuman effort killed him.

"Jolie Blond": This song is so well known in southwest Louisiana that it's referred to as the "Cajun National Anthem." It was also one of the first songs to be recorded when Cajun musicians first came into studios in the late 1920s. The first recording of "Jolie Blond" was titled "Ma Blonde Est Partie (Jolie Blonde)" and was made in 1928 by siblings Amadie, Ophy, and Cleoma Breaux. It tells the sad tale of a man whose heart is broken by a beautiful blond who has left him all alone to lament his fate. Subsequent versions by Leo Soileau and The Hackberry Ramblers (1935) and Harry Choates (1946) helped cement the popularity of this song within Cajun country. As the interest in all things Cajun exploded in the 1980s, so has the song's popularity across the United States.

"K.C. Moan": Related to other songs with similar titles, such as "K.C. Blues," its opening phrase "I thought that I heard that K.C. whistle moan. Blows just like it ain't gonna blow no more" has its roots in a field holler. But "K.C. Moan" became part of the blues tradition, partially through early recordings by The Memphis Jug Band (1927). Its poignant lyrics about the lost love and railroads resonated with later musicians, such as Dave Van Ronk (1967) and Bob Weir and Rob Wasserman (1982), who continued to find personal meaning in this lament.

"Maid Freed from the Gallows": Also known as "Hangman's Song" or "Hangman Tree," this old English ballad found a new home in the United States. Although we don't know how she came to this fate, the song relates the dilemma of a woman who is poised to hang and is anxiously awaiting the payment that will ensure her freedom:

> *Hangman, hangman, slack your rope*
> *Slack it full an' free*
> *For I think I see my Father coming*
> *Away over yonder*
> *Father, O Father, have you brought me gold*
> *Or have you paid my fee*
> *Or have you come to see me hanged*
> *On this green willow tree*

The drama ends only after her father, mother, brother, and sister fail to come through with the money. In the end, her "own true love" rides to her rescue. This dramatic scenario caught the imagination of many twentieth-century American folk musicians from Lead Belly (1935) to Almeda Riddle (1957) to Peter, Paul, and Mary (1965).

"Midnight Special": Artists as diverse as Hoyt Axton (1963), the Limelighter (1963), and The Blue Sky Boys (1965) have recorded this song. The Midnight Special was the train that traveled west out of Houston, Texas, in the early 1920s and roared directly past Sugarland Penitentiary. Now a suburb of Houston, Sugarland was in the country then and housed Huddie Leadbetter (Lead Belly) who, along with other inmates, heard the Midnight Special as a symbol of both freedom from incarceration and the means by which friends and family came to visit. "Midnight Special" is one of the songs that Lead Belly first recorded for the Library of Congress (1934) when he was discovered by Alan and John Lomax at the Angola (Louisiana) Penitentiary while they were on one of their early visits to southern prisons in search of folk music talent.

"Oh Death": "Oh death, won't you spare me over for another year" is the chorus that links the verses of this classic lament about the fate we will all one day meet. "A Conversation with Death" (as it's sometimes called) is a cautionary tale about the time we spend on earth as well as a powerful spiritual wail. First recorded in the late 1920s by a black group, The Pace Jubilee Singers, and shortly thereafter by Delta blues man Charlie Patton and his wife, Bertha Lee, (1934), it regained attention during the folk era by way of recordings by Doc Boggs (1963) and Sarah Ogan Gunning (1965). These versions were sung a cappella as was the version of "Oh Death" sung by Ralph Stanley, which is on the *O Brother, Where Art Thou?* soundtrack. Stanley's version is mournful, lonesome, and compelling.

"Old Joe Clark": A favorite of both old-time string bands and bluegrass ensembles since the late nineteenth century, this tune is well known throughout the United States. "Old Joe Clark" is one of those tunes that works especially well as an instrumental tune for square dancing, examples of which can be heard on early recorded versions by Da Costa Waltz Southern Broadcasters (1927), H. M. Barnes and His Blue Ridge Ramblers (1929), and W. Lee O'Daniel and His Light Crust Doughboys (1935). More recently Pete Seeger recorded it as a banjo solo (1963), and Bill Spence treated it as a hammered dulcimer solo (1973). Collected as early as the late nineteenth century, the nonsense lyrics are peppered with such gems as:

> *I went down to Old Joe's house,*
> *Stayed to have some supper.*
> *Stubbed my toe on the table leg,*
> *And stuck my nose in the butter.*

"Peace in the Valley" (Peace in the Valley, 1938): "Peace in the Valley" is usually thought of as an old gospel song, but it was actually published by the Reverend Thomas A. Dorsey—the onetime blues piano player who turned to gospel in the late 1920s. Since the early 1930s, Dorsey's compositions have been sung in churches across the United States every Sunday, often passed along through oral tradition. They have also found their way into the repertoires of the greatest gospel singers from Mahalia Jackson to The Five Blind Boys of Alabama to Sister Rosetta Tharpe. White artists such as Elvis Presley (1957) and Red Foley (1951) both scored gold records with Dorsey's "(There'll Be) Peace in the Valley."

"Pick a Bale of Cotton":

You gotta jump down, turn around and pick a bale of cotton
Jump down turn around and pick a bale a day
You gotta jump down, turn around and pick a bale of cotton
Jump down turn around and pick a bale a day
Oh, Lawdy, pick-uh-bale-uh-cotton
Oh, Lawdy, pick-uh-bale-uh-day

Along with "Midnight Special," "Grey Goose," and "Goodnight, Irene," this is one of the songs directly connected with Huddie Leadbetter. Like so many of Lead Belly's songs, he plucked it from oral tradition and transformed it to something unique. He often performed it for northern audiences after he left Louisiana and moved to New York City late in 1934. Lead Belly's numerous recordings of "Pick a Bale of Cotton" between 1935 and the late 1940s helped move this song into the ears and minds of many Americans. It was exceptionally popular during the folk revival and recorded by such artists as Harry Belafonte (1956) and The Terriers (1962).

"Poor Boy": This song probably originated among African American singers in the Deep South during Reconstruction, and its chorus "I'm a poor boy, a long ways from home" formed the basis for blues songs that developed at the start of the twentieth century. W. C. Handy recalled hearing it as a boy in Mississippi around 1903, and it was a refrain for songs that Woody Guthrie sang in the 1940s. The black Memphis-based banjo player Gus Cannon (1927) and Kentuckian Buell Kazee (1928) both recorded it early on, while more recently "Poor Boy" was recorded by Doc Watson (1973). Its sentiments of wanderlust, poverty, and loss continue to strike a responsive chord with Americans, including Bob Dylan, whose "Poor Boy Blues" (1962) is certainly informed by "Poor Boy."

"Pretty Polly": Recorded as early as 1926 by old-time Kentucky banjo player John Hammond, this native American ballad relates a tale of deception, treachery, and murder. Willie invites "pretty Polly to come go with me" and after luring her away, Willie then stabs her to death. Ultimately he is caught and "must pay his debt to the devil" for "killing pretty Polly and running away." G. Malcolm Laws included this curious song in his canon of Native American ballads and it was in wide oral circulation as early as the 1890s. Bluegrass bands such as The Stanley Brothers (1950) continued to perform "Pretty Polly," and the song made a comeback during the folk era through recordings by Judy Collins (1968), among others.

"Railroad Bill": Dave Guard and The Whisky Hill Singers (1959) and Joan Baez (1963) were among the folk-based artists who recorded this song during the folk revival. The song is supposedly based on the exploits of Morris Slater, a railroading robber who worked in Tennessee and Alabama in the late 1800s. "Railroad Bill" was first waxed in 1924 by Riley Puckett and the first woman of country music, Roba Stanley; these recordings helped keep the legend alive. Much like a modern version of Robin Hood, this mysterious and interesting figure "never worked and never will," apparently made his living by robbing from the rich, giving to the poor, and then hopping on a freight train to escape.

Red River Valley: With its roots in "A Lady in Love," copywritten by James J. Kerrigan in 1896, this song about lost love and leaving is graced with this sad chorus:

> *Come and sit by my side if you love me,*
> *Do not hasten to bid me adieu,*
> *But remember the Red River Valley,*
> *And the girl that has loved only you.*

"Red River Valley" uses the language of a late-nineteenth-century parlor ballad, which appealed to early country artists such as Carl T. Sprague (1926), Ernest Stoneman and The Dixie Mountaineers (1927), and Harry McClintock (1928), who recorded it under titles such as "Bright Sherman Valley" and "The Cowboy's Love Song." But its melody also influenced other songs that have been transmitted via recordings and oral means. Gene Autry's mega-hit from the early 1930s "Silver Haired Daddy of Mine" and Charlie Poole's influential 1925 recording of "Don't Let Your Deal Go Down" both come from the tune that also underpins "Red River Valley."

"Reuben's Train": A song about a very bad man and the train he should have been on, "Reuben's Train" was recorded as early as 1930 by Emery Arthur and as recently as 1993 by Woodrow Boone and Roger Howell. "Reuben's Train" is most commonly found in the Appalachians among white musicians, though it has also been recorded by black musicians, most notably by Peg Leg Sam (1975):

Ol Reuben made a train and he put it on a track
He ran it to the Lord knows where
Oh me, oh my ran it to the Lord knows where
Should been in town when Reuben's train went down
You could hear that whistle blow 100 miles
Oh me, oh my you could hear the whistle blow 100 miles
I got myself a blade, laid Reuben in the shade,
I'm startin' me a graveyard of my own.
Oh, me, oh lordy my, startin' me a graveyard of my own.

"River of Jordan": Based on a pre–Civil War spiritual, "(I'm Going to Cross the) River of Jordan" has been a favorite among black and white folk musicians for at least 150 years. Its "I'm going down to the river of Jordan one of these days" refrain has echoed through an untold number of black and white country churches since the song emerged. In 1928, The Carter Family included "River of Jordan" on one of their first sessions, while other contemporary artists titled it "Walking on the Streets of Glory." African American artists including Jaybird Coleman, whose plaintive harmonica-vocal rendition (1927) stands in strong contrast to Blind Willie McTell's subdued version for the Library of Congress (1940), have also found solace in this metaphorical song about death and the afterlife.

"Rock Island Line": Although this song is properly associated with Huddie Leadbetter, who recorded it numerous times between 1933 and 1948, The Rooftop Singers (1964) and Barry McGuire with Barry Kane (1974) have also recorded this song. Lead Belly apparently learned the song in the fall of

1934 from prison inmates during a trip through Arkansas with John Lomax in search of folk songs. The precise origins of the song are unknown, but there was a Rock Island Railroad line that ran through Arkansas to Memphis early in the last century. It seems entirely possible "Rock Island Line" might have originated as a work song by black workers clearing out the heavy undergrowth and pine forests of southern Arkansas, while bringing the line east toward Memphis.

"Roll in My Sweet Baby's Arms": Long a bluegrass standard, "Roll in My Sweet Baby's Arms" began its recording history in 1931 when an old-time duo from the North Carolina-Virginia border, Buster Carter and Preston Young, stepped into Columbia's New York City studio. Since then, bluegrass musicians as well known as Lester Flatt and Earl Scruggs (1950) and as obscure as The Barrier Brothers (1977) have included this song as part of their recorded repertoire. This fanciful song about the troubles of love probably comes into bluegrass by way of Bill Monroe. As early as 1937, Bill and Charlie Monroe recorded "Roll in My Sweet Baby's Arms" for Bluebird, and Bill continued to perform the song after forming The Bluegrass Boys in the early 1940s.

"Salty Dog": Songs about rounders, low lives, and no-good men pepper American folk music. Black folk songsters such as Mississippi John Hurt (1964) and traditional bluegrass pickers The Osborne Brothers (1967) have recorded this jaunty, tongue-in-cheek song, which probably dates back to Reconstruction:

> *Standin' on the corner with the low-down blues,*
> *A great big hole in the bottom of my shoes.*
> *Honey, let me be your salty dog.*

Let me be your salty dog,
Or I won't be your man at all.
Honey, let me be your salty dog.

"Sitting on Top of the World": Usually performed as a sixteen-bar blues, this rather mournful song was initially recorded in 1930 by a black string band, The Mississippi Sheiks. Their version sold very well and helped disseminate the song across the country. Its "She may be gone, but I don't worry, 'cause I'm sitting on top of the world" refrain and its musical structure were picked up by western swing outfits like Milton Brown and His Music Brownies (1934) and The Light Crust Doughboys (1938). Its popularity is such that bluegrass musicians as divergent as Curley Fox (1967) and Bill Monroe (1957) also recorded it. Rock musicians, most of whom picked it up from old blues recordings, have not been immune to the song's charms. Cream (1968) recorded one of the best rock versions of this song with Eric Clapton on guitar.

"Streets of Laredo" (Francis Henry Maynard, 1876): This song is a variation of an Irish ballad "A Handful of Laurel," which follows a similar story about a young man dying from an unnamed disease. The immigrants who settled the Appalachians brought with them a version called "The Unfortunate Rake," where the young man lies dying of mercury poisoning, an eighteenth-century treatment for venereal disease. The more adventurous of their descendants brought it with them to Texas, where the lyrics were altered to fit the cowboy life, and his death was caused by gunfire. It also became known under several alternative names, including "The Cowboy's Lament," "The Dying Cowboy," and "Tom Sherman's Barroom." It was a big hit for Marty Robbins in the late 1950s and as early as 1927 by Ewan Hail, Holland Pucket, and Vernon Dalhart.

"This Land Is Your Land" (Woody Guthrie, 1941): Woody Guthrie's Asch recordings from the 1940s are the source of many songs, such as "Do-Re-Me," "Jesus Christ," and "Hard, Ain't It Hard," that not only impressed Bob Dylan but also became standards among folk-based artists in the 1960s. But no song from this period of Guthrie's career had quite the same impact as "This Land Is Your Land," which has appeared in the recorded repertoires of The Limelighters (1962), Pete Seeger (1963), Glen Campbell (1968), and The Country Gentlemen (1973). Guthrie's simple and direct commentary about America's promise, beauty, grandeur has often been called our unofficial national anthem. It's also arguably the best known of our folk-inspired patriotic songs.

"The Titanic": "It was sad when the great ship went down" is the refrain that caught the nation's attention shortly after the sinking of the luxury liner on April 14, 1912, resulting in the death of approximately 1,500 men, women, and children. Within one year of the disaster more than 125 songs about the event were copyrighted, but few of them achieved widespread popularity. The version including the refrain cited above, which is usually titled "The Sinking of the Titanic" or "When That Great Ship Went Down," has emerged as the most enduring. Pioneering traditional artists like Ernest V. Stoneman (1924), William and Versey Smith (1927), and The Cofer Brothers (1927) all recorded similar versions. Furthermore, the song appears in songbooks distributed by the Boy Scouts and has been sung around many a summer camp bonfire over the past nine decades.

"Tom Dooley": This ballad was inspired by the murder of Laura Foster by Thomas C. Dula in Wikles County, North Carolina, in 1866. Dula was captured soon thereafter, tried for the crime, found guilty, and hung on May 1, 1868. Although local musicians G. B. Grayson and Henry Whitter recorded the song from RCA Victor in 1930, it probably would have remained an obscure local murder ballad had song catcher Frank Warner not collected the song from western North Carolina singer Frank Proffitt some eighty years after the event occurred. Alan Lomax included it in his 1948 *Folk Songs, U.S.A.* collection, which later caught the attention of members of The Kingston Trio, who liked it well enough to release it as a single in 1958. The song was so different in its lyric content and musical approach that it caught on immediately and virtually launched the folk revival. Not surprisingly, The Kingston Trio's version inspired many covers such as The Tarriers (1959), The New Lost City Ramblers (1960), and Hank Hill and The Tennessee Folk Trio (1960).

"Wabash Cannonball": The precise origins of this song are unknown, but it first appeared in print in 1904 copyrighted by William Kindt. This version, however, was probably based on an existing train song. Its opening lines about the travel "from the great Atlantic Ocean to the wide Pacific shore" may have inspired Woody Guthrie when he wrote "This Land Is Your Land." "Wabash Cannonball" gained popularity through a 1929 recording by The Carter Family and many subsequent versions give writing credits to A. P. Carter. Roy Acuff adopted "Wabash Cannonball" as his theme in the mid-1930s, which further disseminated the song. It's a song that was not only recorded by early folk artists, but was recorded by more-contemporary folk artists like U. Utah Phillips (1973) and Norman and Nancy Blake (1992) as well as roots-based pop artists such as Wanda Jackson (1959) and the San Francisco psychedelic band The Charlatans (1969).

"We Shall Overcome": With lyrics derived from Charles Tindley's gospel song "I'll Overcome Some Day" (1900), and an opening and closing melody from the nineteenth-century spiritual "No More Auction Block for Me" (a song that predates the Civil War), "We Shall Overcome" became the unofficial anthem for the civil rights movement. It was one of several religious songs of African American origin, along with "We Shall Not Be Moved," adapted for use by civil rights workers. This particular version was apparently reworked by Guy Carawan, Candy Carawan, and a couple of other people associated with the Highlander Research and Education Center, a small progressive non-profit organization based in eastern Tennessee. The Carawans may have picked up the song in the physically remote and mostly black Georgia Sea Islands, where a song like "I'll Overcome Some Day" would have been regularly sung when the couple worked there in the late 1950s. Guy Carawan himself performed it at the 1961 Newport Folk Festival, followed closely by The Freedom Singers (1963) and Joan Baez (1964).

"Where Did You Sleep Last Night?": Sometimes titled "Where Did You Sleep Last Night? (In the Pines)" or "Black Gal, Where Did You Sleep Last Night?" the song dates back to the Reconstruction era. Lead Belly, who recorded it several times between 1935 and 1949, is the apparent source for most of the more contemporary versions of the song, which have been recorded by many pop singers, including Dolly Parton and Connie Francis, as well as grassroots artists like Bill Monroe and The Bluegrass Boys (1977) and Doc Watson (1982).

> *My girl, my girl, don't lie to me*
> *Tell me where did you sleep last night*
> *In the pines, in the pines*

Where the sun don't ever shine
I would shiver the whole night through

This song about deception also caught the attention of Nirvana, particularly its front man, Kurt Cobain. Nirvana played "Where Did You Sleep Last Night?" several times live, most notably on the 1993 MTV Unplugged session in New York, which was released the next year as an album.

"Wildwood Flower": Originally published by J. P. Webster (words) and Maud Irving (music) in 1860, this parlor song is inextricably linked with The Carter Family. This song about love gone wrong, and then lost, is quite sad:

Oh he taught me to love him and called me his flower
A blossom to cheer him through life's weary hour
But now he is gone and left me alone
With the wildflowers to weep and the wild birds to moan

By the time the Carter Family first recorded it (1929), "Wildwood Flower" had long been entered into oral tradition and the public domain. Their version is notable for Sara Carter's soulful vocal and finger-picked guitar accompaniment. The song was little recorded until the folk revival: Joan Baez (1961), Richard Farina (1963), and John McCutcheon (1977) are but a handful of the dozens of musicians who have recorded "Wildwood Flower" since the early 1960s.

"Will the Circle Be Unbroken?" (Ada Habershon and Charles Gabriel, 1907): This semireligious song has strong connections with the civil rights movement, an early 1970s country jam session lead by The Nitty Gritty Dirt Band, and a recent book by Chicago oral historian, radio host, and Pulitzer Prize winner,

Studs Terkel. The lyrics of the song, which was first recorded by The Carter Family in 1935, speaks to the most human condition—death and a return to (depending on your beliefs) heaven or mother earth. The song itself was recorded several more times in the late 1930s: Fisher Hendley and His Aristocratic Pigs (1938) and The Rouse Brothers (1939). But "Will the Circle Be Unbroken?" languished in relative anonymity until The Nitty Gritty Dirt Band focused the hot light of commercial success on it in 1971. The album, which includes appearances by Earl Scruggs, Doc Watson, Merle Travis, Mother Maybelle Carter, Roy Acuff, Jimmy Martin, and Vassar Clements, sold over a million copies during its first two years in release.

"You Are My Sunshine" (Jimmie Davis and Charles Mitchell, 1940): Often perceived to be an older folk tune, this is one of two official songs for the State of Louisiana. It was written by the state's two-time governor, who also recorded such bawdy songs as "Sewing Machine Blues" and "Red Night Gown Blues" some ten years before co-authoring this wildly popular song. "You Are My Sunshine" has been recorded hundreds of times, most notably by Gene Autry (1941), Bing Crosby (1941), and Pete Seeger (1963) since it was initially released in 1940.

SEVEN

Folk Music on CD

S ound recordings have come in many formats, from cylinders to eight-tracks, but today the compact disc is the most viable format for most people who wish to listen to American folk music. Because the recording of American folk music extends back to the late nineteenth century, tens of thousands of recordings could be included here. You may wish to think of the CDs listed in this chapter as a sampling of the broad umbrella under which so many genres reside. But it's a carefully chosen sample that includes many nicely balanced anthologies that cover topics that range from cowboy singers to the folk revival to polka music. You will also find important recordings by important artists such as Bob Dylan and Muddy Waters. While they are not the same thing as being there, these sound recordings offer most listeners the next best thing. All of these compact discs were in print as of the summer of 2004. If you can't find them at your friendly local record store, then they are available at on-line retailers such Amazon, Barnes and Noble, Roots and Rhythm, and Rounder.

The Alan Lomax Collection Sampler, [various artists (Rounder, 1997)]: This release inaugurates a breathtaking reissue series devoted to the work of Alan Lomax on several continents and over fifty years. *The Southern Journey Series* (a thirteen-volume set) revisits the late-1950 recordings by Lomax in the American South. *The Alan Lomax Collection* is—quite literally—all over the map. This 100+ set of well-annotated compact discs looks at his work with folk and vernacular music not only in the United States but also in the Caribbean and Europe.

Anthology of American Folk Music (edited by Harry Smith), various artists (Smithsonian Folkways, 1997): This Grammy award winning, multi-CD set, originally issued in 1952, covers almost every important style of American folk music found in the South and is taken from commercial recordings originally issued during the 1920s through the early 1930s. The selections read almost like a who's who of American folk musicians recording during this period, such as Henry Thomas's "Fishing Blues," Charlie Poole and The North Carolina Ramblers's "White House Blues," and Blind Lemon Jefferson's "Rabbit Foot Blues." This 1997 reissue includes an interactive CD devoted to Harry Smith, the eccentric genius who conceived this highly influential, ground-breaking project.

Arhoolie Records 40th Anniversary Collection: The Journey of Chris Strachwitz, various artists (Arhoolie, 2000): This five-CD set and lavish booklet celebrates the label and the work of its founder, Chris Strachwitz, with a well-rounded anthology of his field recordings of blues, conjunto, string bands, etc., presented in chronological order. Lightnin' Hopkins, Mance Lipscomb, and Clifton Chenier are just three of the important artists who appear on this varied and delightful set.

Back in the Saddle Again, various artists (New World, 1999): This is a well-executed package two-CD set that samples a wide range of cowboy music. It includes performances by a variety of artists from the 1920s through the 1940s such as Gene Autry, The Sons of the Pioneers, Patsy Montana, Jimmie Rodgers, and The Girls of the Golden West. A nicely designed and immensely readable booklet enhances the usefulness of this set.

The Best of Broadside 1962–1988: Anthems of the American Underground from the Pages of *Broadside* Magazine, various artists (Smithsonian Folkways, 2000): *Broadside* magazine was at the vortex of the folk-based protest music scene in New York City in the early 1960s. It published articles about local and national artists as well as new songs by artists such as Phil Ochs, Tom Paxton, and Bob Dylan. This elaborate five-CD set comes with a comprehensive booklet that highlights and underscores the importance of the protest music documented and disseminated by this magazine.

Borderlands: From Conjunto to Chicken Scratch, various artists (Smithsonian Folkways, 1993): A sampler of the Hispanic American grassroots music found along the Mexico-U.S. border and marked by the Rio Grande. Oscar Hernandez, Narciso Martinez, and Lydia Mendoza are among the musicians performing the polkas, corridos, and (old and new) styles of chicken scratch that constitute the vernacular music along this extensive and very fluid cultural line.

Captain, Captain, Mance Lipscomb (Arhoolie, 1998): These are among the best early (mid-1960s) recordings by the important Texas-born African American songster. This set includes a wide range of material, such as blues ("Easy Rider Blues"), country dance tunes ("Heel and Toe Polka"), ballads ("Frankie and Albert"), and topical songs ("Segregation Done Past"), which are the hallmark of a man who played at country dances in Texas in the 1930s and on college campuses in the 1970s.

The Carter Family on Border Radio, The Carter Family (Arhoolie, 1995-1999): The 1939 transcriptions from radio stations that blasted into the United States from just over the border in Mexico are the original source material for these three CDs. The material is the usual mix of sentimental songs, ballads, and Carter Family standards, such as "Cyclone of Rye Cove," "Worried Man Blues," and "River of Jordan." You get to hear the informality of a radio program as well as their theme song. The line up of performers is a bit different from that on their commercial records from this period, thus providing a fresh look at this important musical family.

The Complete Plantation Recordings, Muddy Waters (MCA, 1993): Unlike the brazen, amplified Chicago blues that sprung forth in the late 1940s, this acoustic set contains Waters's complete Library of Congress recordings from the early 1940s. These are his earliest recordings, and you can hear him playing solo (a la Robert Johnson) on versions of "I Be's Troubled" and "Country Blues." MCA wisely decided to include the interview material, which rounds out this portrait of Muddy as a Delta blues man.

Complete Recordings of Robert Johnson, Robert Johnson (Columbia, 1990): These forty-one recordings constitute the oeuvre of this influential Mississippi Delta blues man whose music is now revered as among the finest country blues recordings ever made. Johnson recorded the first versions of songs such as "Sweet Home Chicago," "From Four Until Late," "Stop Breaking Down," and "I Believe I'll Dust My Broom," which have gone on to be re-recorded hundreds of times by blues and blues-influenced musicians as diverse as Elmore James and Eric Clapton.

Corridos y Narcocorridos, various artists (Fonovisa, 2001): The corridos (Mexican ballad) tradition goes back to the 1800s, with stories about heroes and bad men. But in the late twentieth century, the tradition turned its attention to a vigorous business that thrived along the Mexico-U.S. border: the trafficking of narcotics. From the 1980s to the present, narcocorridos became the most important form of ballad in the region, and this release highlights some of the best from this genre such as "Contrabando y Traición" (Smuggling and betrayal) by Los Tigres del Norte, "Masacre en el Charco" (Massacre in el Charco) by Los Pajaritos del Sur, and "Violencia en Los Angeles" (Violence in Los Angeles) by Pedro Rivera. This set is enhanced by Elijah Wald's fine notes, which are partially derived from his 2001 book on the subject, *Narcocorrido: A Journey into the Music of Drugs, Guns, and Guerrillas.*

Crossroads, Southern Routes: Music of the American South (Enhanced CD), various artists (Smithsonian Folkways, 1996): This deftly crafted interactive CD surveys music from the South, including blues, gospel, bluegrass, Cajun, and many of the other genres covered in the book. The selections are largely drawn from the vast Smithsonian Folkways catalog and include fine performances by Brownie McGhee, Bill Monroe, Doc Watson, and Dewey Balfa.

Deep Polka: Dance Music from the Midwest, various artists (Smithsonian Folkways, 1998): These twenty-six contemporary selections include German, Danish, Finnish, Czech, Croatian, and Norwegian bands from the upper Midwest. The combination of a lucid, informative booklet with sterling performances like the "Mountaineer Polka" by Norm Dombrowski's Happy Notes and "Minnesota Polka" by Karl and The Country Dutchmen make this the best introduction to Midwest polka music.

Early Roanoke Country Radio, various artists (Global Village, 1997): An extensive booklet accompanies this set, which covers the period between 1925 and 1955, when music on the radio was mostly performed by live musicians in the studio. For a city in the Blue Ridge Mountains, a surprising number of groups are heavily influenced by western swing instead of the older mountain tunes and bluegrass that one would expect. A complete fifteen-minute program by Roy Hall and The Blue Ridge Entertains is perhaps the highlight of this release.

The Early Years: 1958–1962, New Lost City Ramblers (Smithsonian Folkways, 1991): This repackaging of the best of The New Lost City Ramblers influential work was carefully chosen in collaboration with the artists. Included are topical songs ("How Can a Poor Man Stand Such Times and Live?"), old-time string band standards ("Don't Let Your Deal Go Down"), and country standards ("Brown's Ferry Blues"). This is as good a sampling of The New Lost City Ramblers as can be found on CD today.

Fifteen Early Tejano Classics, various artists (Arhoolie, 1998): This sampler of rancheros, polkas, and boleros was originally recorded for small, border labels between the mid-1940s and the late 1950s. This disc underscores the variety of music documented by commercial companies for an indigenous audience in an attempt to hit it big. Included are some of the first recordings by Freddy Fender and Tony de la Rosa as well as a stirring performance by Lydia Mendoza.

The First Ten Years, Joan Baez (Vanguard, 1990): More than any current release, this one focuses on Baez's protest and folk-based songs like "Hard Rain's a-Gonna Fall" and "John Riley." These are the songs that placed Baez into the limelight and remain among her strongest performances. A few of the songs, most notably "With God on Our Side," are still timely and relevant forty years after Baez first recorded them.

Flaco's First, Flaco Jimenez (Arhoolie, 1995): These are among the first commercial recordings by this pioneering figure of conjunto accordion playing. They first appeared on small labels in the mid-1950s and reached a small but loyal audience. Now you can enjoy strong performances of songs such as "Corazon Humano" or "Raquel Polka" without searching high and low for the rare original recordings.

Folk Masters: Great Performances Recorded Live at the Barns of Wolf Trap, various artists (Smithsonian Folkways, 1993): A compilation from the public radio series of the same name, these performances came from the 1992 season and include such stalwarts as Dewey Balfa, the Texas Playboys, Cephas and Wiggins, and Boozoo Chavis. Taken together, this compact disc serves as a nice introduction to a wide range of genres, including blues, Cajun, zydeco, and western swing. Nick Spitzer, who produced this record and contributed the notes, is also the host of *American Routes,* a weekly grassroots music program heard across the United States over Public Radio International's network.

Forever: An Anthology, Judy Collins (Elektra/Asylum, 1997): This is a nice two-CD retrospective that covers most of Judy Collins's career beginning with folk-based selections such as "Maid of Constant Sorrow" and "In the Hills of Shiloh." Sprinkled through the disc are more heavily orchestrated numbers, including "Send in the Clowns" and "Pirate Jenny." Collins never limited herself to folk music, per say, but this anthology certainly exposes her roots.

Freedom: The Golden Gate Quartet & Josh White at the Library of Congress, various artists (Bridge, 2002): Alan Lomax's fingerprints are all over this fascinating release. In the late 1930s Lomax was promoting folk music via recordings, radio, and live performances, and The Golden Gate Quartet was his favorite group at the time. This 1940 live performance of blues, gospel, and work songs was recorded at the Library of Congress and features not only music but also commentary by Alan Lomax and the noted poet Sterling Brown.

Freight Train and Other North Carolina Folk Songs and Tunes, Elizabeth Cotten (Smithsonian Folkways, 1989): "Freight Train" is certainly her best known song, but your life will be richer for hearing Cotten's versions of "Graduation March," "Ain't Got No Honey Babe Now," and "Going Down That Road Feeling Bad." Her music is gentle, lyrical, and betrays her roots in the music heard in the late nineteenth century.

Gaither Gospel Series, The Statesmen (Chordant, 1997): The Statesmen are among the premier southern gospel groups, with a heritage that goes back to the late 1940s. They incessantly toured the South during the 1950s and 1960s, which marked the height of their popularity. This compact disc of vintage performances includes strong versions of "Get away Jordan," "I'm Climbing Higher and Higher," and "Up above My Head."

Georgia Sea Island Songs, various artists (New World, 1992): This anthology contains a mixture of sacred and secular material from this musically conservative community, which was overlooked by most researchers until after World War II. Bessie Jones is the matriarch of the group, though John Davis is probably the strongest singer. Their repertoire includes songs like "Buzzard Lope" that recall a time when African Americans were not free.

Go 'Long Mule, Uncle Dave Macon (County, 1995): One of country music's greatest entertainers, Uncle Dave Macon did not begin his professional career until he was fifty years old. Beginning in the mid-1920s he recorded extensively and appeared on the *Grand Ole Opry* for many years. We are fortunate that County Records has reissued some of his best work here, including some of his strongest Fruit Jar Drinkers selections: "Sail away Ladies," "Rabbit in the Pea Patch," and "Jordan Am a Hard Road to Travel."

The Gospel Ship: Baptist Hymns and White Spirituals from the Southern Mountains, various artists (New World, 1994): A balanced collection based on Alan Lomax's field recordings from the late 1950s, this set documents a variety of older religious songs. Most of them are solo selections and the strongest are by Texas Gladden (better known as a ballad singer) and Hobart Smith. The small group recordings by The Mountain Ramblers underscore the relationship between bluegrass and gospel. It's a good introduction to sacred music that blossomed in the early twentieth century.

Hank Williams's Health and Happiness Shows, Hank Williams (Mercury, 1993): Williams is a legend in country music and a big influence on musicians ranging from Bob Dylan to Wilco. This double compact disc provides eight complete twelve-minute radio programs originally broadcast in the fall of 1949 that include a surprising number of older fiddle tunes such as "Sally Goodin" as well as Williams's theme song for these Hadacol-sponsored broadcasts, "Happy Roving Cowboy." These are at least as strong as his MGM recordings and reveal a side of Williams and The Drifting Cowboys that rarely came across in his later years. The insightful notes by Colin Escott are another strength of this important release.

Hawaiian Drum Dance Chants: Sounds of Power in Time, various artists (Smithsonian Folkways, 1992): Although its not definitive, this compact disc provides you with a wide range of chants, both solo and accompanied by dancers and percussion, recorded between 1923 and 1989. Some of the early recordings, which were supplied by Honolulu's Bishop Museum, offer a glimpse back to the nineteenth century, while the first six tracks are actually more contemporary hula pahu songs.

Honor the Earth Pow-Wow: Songs of the Great Lakes Indians, various artists (Rykodisc, 1992): This compact disc documents the 1990 gathering of the same name, which attracted members of the Ojibwa, Menominee, and Winnebago tribes from Wisconsin and Minnesota. These intertribal celebrations honor Mother Earth through a combination of singing, dancing, and drumming. The songs touch on a number of themes, including a song composed for a son serving overseas in the air force during World War II, which exemplifies a tradition of war songs sung for protection before battle.

If I Had a Hammer: Songs of Hope and Struggle, Pete Seeger (Smithsonian Folkways, 1998): This retrospective collects some of Seeger's best topical material onto one compact disc. The notes emphasize the songs' origins, many of which have roots in progressive political causes that Seeger has championed his entire adult life. Some of the best of these songs, such as "Turn, Turn, Turn," "Where Have All the Flowers Gone," and "Which Side Are You On?" have found a wide audience from summer camps to college campuses.

In Concert: Peter Paul & Mary, Peter, Paul, and Mary (Warner Brothers, 1990): From a 1964 concert, this is strong vintage material that captures their easy stage banter and nicely performed material that ranges from "The Times They Are a' Changing" to Blind Gary Davis's "If I Had My Way." It's a fun session that illustrates how groups like Peter, Paul, and Mary seamlessly blended religious songs, children's material, and protest material to an appreciative audience that enjoyed their eclectic repertoire.

King Biscuit Time, Sonny Boy Williams (Arhoolie, 1993): From well-seasoned entertainer and blues harpist, these are the classic early selections by Sonny Boy Williamson number two (a.k.a. Willie Williams or Rice Miller). In the Deep South, he made his mark broadcasting over KFFA in West Helena, Arkansas, which lead him to record these selections for Trumpet Records in Jackson, Mississippi, before he joined the Great Migration to Chicago in the early 1950s. These are some of the best electrified (and electrifying) down-home blues recordings; just listen to "Mighty Long Time" if you are at all skeptical!

La Musique Creole, various artists (Arhoolie, 1996): Although it's not listed as such, this is really a showcase for the considerable talents of the French African American musician Alphonse "Bois Sec" Ardoin. He plays old-style zydeco music, which is very closely related to its Cajun counterpart, and this music provides the roots for more modern players like Rockin' Dupsie. "Allons Danser" and "Ardoin Two Step" provide the highlights of this spirited release.

Ladies and Gentlemen . . . The Grateful Dead: Fillmore East April 1971, The Grateful Dead (Arista, 2000): A typical Dead recording from this period (though with second drummer Mickey Hart absent for the gig) includes many of the group's originals, such as "China Cat Sunflower" and "Dark Star" among the selections. What sets this gig apart from others is Pigpen's blues shouting on standards such as "I'm a King Bee" and "It Hurts Me Too" as well as their inclusion of more folk-based material than usual: "Going Down the Road Feeling Bad," "New Minglewood Blues," "Casey Jones," and "Dark Hollow."

Lead Belly's Last Sessions, Lead Belly (Smithsonian Folkways, 1994): Because these recordings were made while Lead Belly was fighting the effects of Lou Gehrig's disease, they are not as musically strong as other Asch and Folkways releases. Nonetheless, this four-CD boxed set is one of his most interesting and revealing due to its informal nature and the stories that he relates. *Last Sessions* does include good performances of Lead Belly's favorites ("Midnight Special," "The Grey Goose," "Rock Island Line," and "Irene") as well as thoughtful booklet notes.

Lydia Mendoza—The First Queen of Tejano Music, Lydia Mendoza (Arhoolie, 1996): A retrospective of this important Tejano singer-guitarist, this collection samples her early work. Mendoza first recorded with her family in the late 1920s and continued her career as a solo artist beginning in the mid-1930s. Most of these records feature her distinctive voice and solo guitar accompaniment on impassioned selections such as "Vi Pasar" and "Amor En Duda."

Mariachi Tapatío de José Marmolejo—Mexico's Pioneer Mariachis, Volume 2, Mariachi Tapatio (Arhoolie, 1996): Mariachi Tapatio was at one time the most popular group in Mexico. They were featured in a number of films, played on the ultra-high-powered Mexican radio stations, and made many recordings. These recordings are from around 1937 and helped legitimize the trumpet as a featured instrument in mariachi orchestras. Good notes and pioneering folk-based music make this one to seek out.

Masters of the Delta Blues: The Friends of Charlie Patton, various artists (Yazoo, 1991): If you wish to spend over $100 on a Delta blues reissue, then you should invest in Revenent's unparalleled, multi-Grammy-award-winning box set *The Worlds of Charlie Patton*. If that is too pricey, this set will more than do to introduce you to the genre. Virtually every track, most of which were recorded in the late 1920s or early 1930s, is a certified classic. The quality of all of the selections by the likes of Eddie "Son" House, Tommy Johnson, and Ishman Bracey makes it difficult to highlight individual performances, but the fact that Yazoo has included three previously unissued Paramount test pressings makes this an essential release.

Mexican-American Border Music, Volume 1: Pioneer Recording Artists (1928–1958), various artists (Arhoolie, 1994): The first album in Arhoolie's superb Tex-Mex series traces the roots of the modern accordion-based norteño-Tejano-conjunto sound that developed in the late 1930s. Important figures such as blind fiddler El Ciego Melquiades, the omni-present Lydia Mendoza, and accordion pioneers Santiago Jiménez and Narciso Martinez are among the featured artists. An exceptionally well written thirty-six-page booklet contextualizes the music and helps make this a strong contender for the best set of Tex-Mex border music yet issued.

Mississippi: River of Song—A Musical Journey down the Mississippi, various artists (Smithsonian Folkways, 1998): A musical tour of the Mississippi River is the focus of this two-CD set that accompanies a four-part PBS television series of the same name. *River of Song* celebrates not only the physical landscapes through which the water traverses but also the colorful Native American, Dutch, African American, and Cajun cultures that have sprung from and thrive along the river. Significantly, this release does justice to the religious music the producers encountered along the way.

The Music of Bill Monroe from 1936–1994, Bill Monroe (MCA, 1994): This four-CD set, which comes with a very helpful booklet, offers the best survey of Monroe's lengthy career. It begins with a Monroe Brothers duet ("My Long Journey Home"), continues with proto-bluegrass ("Heavy Traffic Ahead"), documents the early classic recordings ("Uncle Pen"), and concludes with the elder statesman of bluegrass ("Pike County Breakdown"). This is an essential release for anyone with any interest in bluegrass.

My Rough and Rowdy Ways, Volumes 1 and 2, various artists (Yazoo, 1998): These two compact discs survey songs about "bad men and hellraisers." The forty-six selections were originally recorded during the 1920s and 1930s by artists such as Uncle Dave Macon, Tommy Johnson, The Fruit Jar Guzzlers, and Ken Maynard. They explore a variety of themes, including drugs (Will Shade on "Better Leave That Stuff Alone"), gambling (Clifford Gibson on "Bad Luck Dice"), robbery (Carolina Buddies on "Otto Wood the Bandit"), and alcoholism (Big Bill on "Good Liquor Gonna Carry Me Down").

Nashville Skyline / New Morning / John Wesley Harding, Bob Dylan (Columbia/Sony, 1997): Columbia has conveniently packaged these three important early to middle 1960s folk, country, rock albums by the most influential artist in the genre. These albums contain some of Dylan's most important early work, "John Wesley Harding" and "I Am a Lonesome Hobo." It also includes his controversial "country" period, which is exemplified by "Lay, Lady, Lay" and his duet with Johnny Cash "Girl from the North Country."

No Depression (original recording remastered; extra tracks), Uncle Tupelo (Columbia/Legacy, 2003): All of the recordings by Uncle Tupelo, which was fronted by Jeff Tweedy and Jay Farrar, are worth listening to, but this one—their first—matters the most. This expanded edition includes a previously unissued 1988 demo version of the title track as well as a previously unissued 1987 version of "Blues Die Hard." The sound on the album is improved, which makes songs such as "Graveyard Shift" and "Flatness" sound even better!

Non-Blues Secular Black Music in Virginia, various artists (Global Village, 1995): A nicely annotated sampling of field and commercial recordings made between the mid-1930s and the mid-1970s. Instead of focusing on the more familiar blues tradition, this release explores the vibrant, important (and often overlooked) protest songs, string-band instrumentals, ballads, and country dance tunes that were widely performed by black folk musicians in the Commonwealth of Virginia.

O Brother, Where Art Thou?, various artists (Polygram 2000): This best-selling soundtrack to the Coen Brothers' quirky film has helped introduce a new generation to grassroots music. The soundtrack contains fine performances by artists as well known as Alison Krauss and as obscure as J. Carter. Music producer T-Bone Burnett has included a work song ("Po Lazarus" by J. Carter and Prisoners), blues (" Hard Time Killing Floor Blues" by Chris Thomas King), and gospel bluegrass ("Angel Band" by The Stanley Brothers) among the selections.

Oh My Little Darling: Folk Song Types, various artists (New World, 2002): This anthology emphasizes the variety of folk music found on sound recordings from across the South. The genres include a ballad of British origins ("King William Was King George's Son" by Mr. and Mrs. Crockett Ward), a cowboy song ("Whoopee-Ti-Yi-Yo" by John I. White), a topical song ("Come All You Coal Miners" by Sarah Ogan), and a stirring Pentecostal church performance ("If the Light Has Gone out in Your Soul" by Ernest Phipps and His Holiness Singers). Given the quality of the selections and the quality of the annotations, this single disc is hard to beat.

Old-Time Fiddle Tunes and Songs from North Georgia, Gid Tanner and The Skillet Lickers (County, 1996): Here are sixteen of the finest old-time string-band recordings from the middle to late 1920s. Gideon Tanner and his talented crew, which featured Riley Puckett on guitar and vocal along with fiddlers Lowe Stokes and Tanner, performed some of the most raucous and giddy fiddle tunes and songs ever committed to record. Who wouldn't have loved to be in the studio when they recorded "Hell Broke Loose in Georgia!"?

Old Time O'odham Fiddle Music, various artists (Canyon, 1997): This is the first widely available commercial recording of this unique genre, which is performed by the Tohono O'odham people of southern Arizona. This utterly delightful and archaic sounding ensemble utilizes violins, guitar, and drums to play a variety of polkas, two-steps, and mazurkas. This is fiddle music that sounds utterly unlike anything else in the United States.

The Rough Guide to Klezmer, various artists (World Music Network, 2000): Meant as a companion to the book of the same name, this anthology does a nice job of surveying klezmer. The compiler both pays attention to pioneers such as Naftule Brandwein and acknowledges the role that groups such as The Flying Bulgar Klezmer Band, The Klezmer Conservatory Band, and Klezmokum have done to preserve and disseminate this music. It's impossible to definitively sample klezmer on a single compact disc, but this one comes close.

Smithsonian Folkways American Roots Collection, various artists (Smithsonian Folkways, 1996): These twenty-six tracks can't possibly cover all of the musical categories released by Smithsonian Folkways. But it does encompass most of the important folk and folk-based genres, and the artists range from Lead Belly to Lucinda Williams to Pete Seeger to Bill Monroe.

Times Ain't Like They Used to Be: Early American Rural Music—Volumes 1-4, various artists (Yazoo, 1997–1999): An eclectic collection of some of the best recordings of blues, rags, fiddle tunes, ballads, and more from the 1920s and 1930s by artists as diverse as Henry Thomas, Fiddlin' John Carson, the Reverend D. C. Rice, and The Shelor Family. Compiler Richard Nevins has selected some of the best performances by these rural (mostly southern) folk musicians.

Tommy & Fred: Best Fiddle-Banjo Duets played by Tommy Jarrell and Fred Cockerham, Tommy Jarrell and Fred Cockerham (County, 1994): Surry County, North Carolina, is one of the strongholds for old-time string band music and these two men come from families whose roots in the music extend back to the late 1800s. These recordings were made when Jarrell and Cockerham were in their sixties, and their versions of fiddle and banjo duets such as "Sally Ann," "Breaking Up Christmas," "John Brown's Dream," and "Old Bunch of Keys" are simply classics.

Traditional Voices, various artists (Canyon, 1998): Canyon Records is one of the oldest company's documenting Native American music, and this anthology samples Canyon's extensive early (early 1950s through the middle 1960s) catalog. It presents music from twenty tribes, most of which are located in the Southwestern United States, but it does include groups from as far afield as North Dakota and Canada. The selections include Lakota love songs, Hopi dances, and Dakota grass songs.

Traveling through the Jungle: Fife and Drum Bands from the Deep South, various artists (Hightone/Testament, 1995): This compilation includes selections from western Georgia and its stronghold in the hill country of Mississippi. This fascinating African American tradition was first documented by Alan Lomax for the Library of Congress in 1941 and some of these early recordings (most notably "Jesse James" by The Sid Hemphill Band) are included here. Most of the selections, however, are of later field recordings by Napoleon Strickland and Othar Turner.

Wade in the Water—African American Sacred Music Traditions, various artists (Smithsonian Folkways, 1997): A four-CD set, each of which can be purchased separately, focuses on four distinct traditions: spirituals performed in the concert tradition, congregational singing, community groups, and gospel. This music formed the core of an award-winning series that Bernice Reagon Johnson produced for National Public Radio. *Wade in the Water* is a very thorough and enjoyable introduction to the variety of folk-based black religious singing heard in churches throughout the United States in the late twentieth century.

Washington Square Memories—The Great Urban Folk Boom, 1950–1970, various artists (Rhino, 2001): These three CDs contain performances by musicians associated with the urban folk scene in New York City just before and after the folk boom swept the United States in the early 1960s. The artists include a diverse cast of characters as zany as The Holy Model Rounders and as grounded as Tom Paxton. You will also hear fine performances by Joan Baez, Tim Buckley, Peggy Seeger, Bob Dylan, Bud and Travis, and Hedy West. All told this is a well conceived and nicely annotated package.

Woody Guthrie—The Asch Recordings Volumes 1–4, Woody Guthrie (Smithsonian Folkways, 1997–1999): These four CDs, each of which is thoroughly annotated, contain some of Guthrie's finest early (late 1930s through the 1940s) recordings. If you are looking for the classic recordings by Guthrie, you will find very fine (perhaps even definitive) versions of "So Long, Its Been Good to Know You," "Vigilante Man," "Pretty Boy Floyd," "Do-Re-Mi," and "Philadelphia Lawyer" on these discs. The discs are available as a box set or individually; if you are fiscally challenged, "This Land Is Your Land" is the one to get.

Yiddish-American Klezmer Music 1925–1926, Davd Tarras (Yazoo, 1992): A compelling retrospective of Dave Tarras's long and distinguished career, this release underscores the variety of music that came under the rubric of Klezmer music. The later selections betray the influence of jazz and swing, while the earliest cuts reveal its roots in old-world types such as doynas, freilekhs, and horas. Whatever the genre, Tarras was a master clarinet player, and the richness and diversity of his legacy constitutes the heart of this fine compilation.

Young Fogies—Volumes 1 and 2, various artists (Rounder, 1994–1995): The liner notes here observe that these anthologies under-score "the diverse and potent traditional music found in America." To this description I would add that it's a mixture of younger and more veteran musicians performing mostly old-time selections with dashes of other grassroots music peppered throughout. The musicianship is high and the tunes lively. All told, this is a fine tribute to the older music and the musicians that the younger folks helped to perpetuate.

Zydeco, Volume 1: The Early Years: 1961–1962, various artists (Arhoolie, 1988): This is raw, unadorned, down-home zydeco music, most of which was recorded by Arhoolie maven Chris Strachwitz, at house parties and beer joints in Houston and southwest Louisiana. Most of the artists were local, non-professionals, such as Albert Chevalier and Willie Green, who worked at day jobs and performed at small clubs in the evenings. Zydeco king and professional accordion player Clifton Chenier is the notable exception to this observation, and the release contains a reissue of his first commercial R&B-style recording from the mid-1950s. With this and one other reissue from 1949, why it was titled *The Early Years, 1961–1962* remains a mystery to me!

EIGHT

The Language of American Folk Music

A & R (artist and repertoire) man: The company employee who scouts talent and assists with selecting the artist's repertoire to be recorded.

A cappella: Performed without instrumental accompaniment.

Acoustic: An instrumental (or a vocal performance) that does not use electrical amplification.

Air shot: A recording of a radio broadcast.

Antiphony: Also known as call and response, this technique features a leader who calls and a group or an individual who responds. Shape-note singing uses antiphony—it's also one of the hallmarks of African American folk music.

Arranger: The person who figures out the parts (voices or instruments) performed by an ensemble.

Ballad: Any song that tells a story.

Beat: The basic metric unit of music—it's what you tap your feet to!

Boogie-woogie: A style of blues piano that developed in the 1920s and features strongly pronounced bass figures in the left hand.

Bottleneck guitar: The use of a metal or glass slide to play the guitar, which was often used by blues guitarists such as Muddy Waters and Robert Johnson.

Broadside: A composed and published ballad, often from seventeenth- to nineteenth-century England, which sometimes became part of oral tradition.

Child ballad: One of sixteenth- to nineteenth-century British ballads that was cataloged by Harvard English professor Francis James Child.

Chord: A combination of at least three notes played simultaneously.

Claw-hammer banjo: A style of banjo playing (also called frailing) that is particularly strong in the southern Appalachians and is integral to old-time music ensembles. Grandpa Jones, Uncle Dave Macon, and Wade Ward are three banjo players who use this style of playing.

Crossover: A performance or performer who is well known in one field but who attracts attention in another. The Dixie Chicks, for example, have a following in country music (and strong bluegrass roots) but have also sold well in the pop music field.

Dynamics: Changes in loudness or feeling within a musical piece.

Ethnomusicology: The scholarly study of musical culture outside of the Western classical tradition.

Gig: Any musical engagement held at a bar, small club, large festival, and so on.

Fais do-do: A music and dance party in Cajun country that begins at night after the children have gone to bed.

Fiddle tune: A tune associated with the repertoire of an old-time fiddler, which is sometimes transposed to either banjo or guitar.

Finger picking: A guitar style, utilized by guitarists as diverse as Merle Travis and Blind Blake, in which the fingers emphasize the melody and the thumb provides the bass line.

Flat picking: A style of guitar and mandolin playing that uses a plectrum (a pick) to strum or rapidly pick out single notes. Doc Watson and Bill Monroe are two examples of flat pickers.

Front line: The featured or lead instruments in a group, such as the banjo, fiddle, and mandolin in a bluegrass ensemble.

Gospel: Any style of black or white religious (folk) music that is composed.

Harp: Another name for a harmonica.

Intonation: The ability of a musician to perform or sing in tune, particularly with others.

Jig: A spirited dance tune in 6/8 time.

Jug band: A novelty musical ensemble, such as The Memphis Jug Band, featuring a resonating instrument, such as a stovepipe or whiskey jug. Jug bands were particularly popular in the 1920s and 1930s.

Lyric song: A song with words that do not tell a narrative story. Blues is one of the best examples of a lyric folk song.

Lyrics: The words of a song.

Matachine: A music, drama, dance, and religious ceremony held by Pueblo Indians, usually on New Year's Day.

Melisma: A musical passage in which several notes are sung to the same syllable.

Modes: Scales that are neither major nor minor, which makes certain fiddle tunes (for example) sound "archaic."

Ornamentation: Embellishments of the line of a melody.

Ostinato: A short repeated phrase or figure.

Pitch: The high or low quality of a tone.

Polka: An instrumental selection in 2/4 time.

Public domain: Songs or tunes that are not copyrighted, which is true for most American folk music.

Reel: A dance tune, often with Celtic roots, that is usually played in 4/4 time.

Rhythm section: The group of musicians (typically bass, rhythm guitar, and percussion) whose primary function is to provide a rhythmic, metrical, and harmonic foundation.

Rockabilly: An early form of rock 'n' roll, which is rooted in country music, blues, and R&B.

Sanctified: Musical practices associated with Pentecostal churches.

Shape note: A style of sacred singing found mostly in New England and the South, where the pitch is indicated by the shape of the note.

Sideman: Musicians who are hired by the leader of the band.

Slack-key guitar: By the late 1880s, some Hawaiian guitarists, including the legendary Joseph Kukuku, were tuning their guitars to a major triad and playing a style with a slide that produced a unique sound. This style became influential on the mainland, when a fad for Hawaiian music began in 1915. White and black American folk musicians heard this music and embraced the basic concept of playing an open-tuned guitar with a slide.

Solo: The point at which a musician steps forward to play on his or her own.

Songster: African American rural performers—such as John Jackson, Pink Anderson, Mance Lipscomb, and Lead Belly—who perform blues, field hollers, ballads, religious songs, and country dance tunes. Songsters typically accompany themselves on string instruments, usually a guitar or a banjo.

Syncopation: The shift in accent to a beat that would normally be "weak," for example, emphasizing beats 2 and 4 in 4/4 time.

Tempo: The rate (or speed) at which the beat is played.

Timbre: The unique "color" or sound of a particular instrument, voice, or ensemble.

Topical song: A song that delivers a social commentary or message.

Trainer: In the African American gospel quartet tradition, this is the person who works out arrangements, assigns vocal ranges, and assists with repertoire.

Triple meter: Any rhythm (or meter) that can be divided by three, most commonly 3/4 or 6/8.

Verse: This is the section that precedes the chorus. Many American folk songs follow the verse, chorus, verse format.

Vibrato: Describes the alteration of pitch, usually in a voice of reed instrument, that is often used as an expressive device.

Waltz: A song or instrumental performance in 3/4 time.

Resources for Curious Listeners

While books, magazines, and video material cannot substitute for experiencing music "live," they remain invaluable tools for anyone interested in American traditional music. The reasons are largely practical—enough of this music is in the distant past (how many people are around today to discuss their firsthand experiences performing at a fiddler's contest in the 1920s?) or too geographically remote (the majority of Americans live nowhere near a Tohono O'odham Reservation in order to hear chicken scratch music in context!) to be reasonably accessible. This chapter, while not comprehensive, suggests some of the best resources for the further exploration of American folk music.

Books

A book or monograph can describe musical cultures in a way that might not be readily apparent. It provides more in-depth information than even the best notes that accompany a sound recording or a teacher's guide for a video documentary. Books may appear old-fashioned in today's world, but no medium has yet to supercede them for conveying factual information to a wide audience.

American Roots Music, edited by Robert Santelli: Compiled from interviews, photographs, and essays, Santelli edited this volume, which explores the history of American vernacular music; it's the companion to the 2001 PBS television series.

Barrio Rhythm: Mexican American Music in Los Angeles, Steven Loza: This is a look at the varieties of vernacular musics that underscore the interaction between genres such as conjunto with more modern, popular styles.

Big Road Blues, David Evans: Evans presents a scholarly, in-depth examination of musical creativity in the central Mississippi blues tradition.

Bluegrass: A History, Neil V. Rosenberg: Although more than a decade has passed since its publication, Rosenberg's book remains the best for detailing the history of this post–World War II genre.

Can't Be Satisfied: The Life and Times of Muddy Waters, Robert Gordon: At last, here's a thorough and insightful biography of one of the world's most influential and interesting blues men.

Down the Highway: The Life of Bob Dylan, Howard Sounes: Based on extensive interviews and oral histories with Dylan's friends and family, this book helps illuminate his life like never before.

Folk Music in America: A Reference Guide, Terry Miller: Miller provides a valuable guide to articles, books, and other studies of

American grassroots music published through the middle 1980s.

The Folk Music Sourcebook, 2nd ed, Larry Sandberg and Dick Weissman: With sections titled "Listening," "Learning," "Playing," and "Hanging Out," this book covers nearly everything in contemporary American folk music.

Good Friends and Bad Enemies: Robert Winslow Gordon and the Study of American Folksong, Debora Kodish: This is a study of the life and times of Robert W. Gordon, folk song collecting, and the early days of the Archive of Folk Song at the Library of Congress.

A Good Natured Riot: The Story of The Grand Ole Opry, Charles K. Wolfe: This is the definitive study of the development of *The Grand Ole Opry*, with a strong focus on its early years.

Woody Guthrie: A Life, Joe Klein: This is the best biography yet written on the life and music of Woody Guthrie.

How Sweet the Sound: The Golden Age of Gospel, Horace Boyer: This is a survey of gospel music focusing on the 1920s through the 1960s.

Introducing American Folk Music: Grassroots and Ethnic Music in the United States, Kip Lornell: This textbook is aimed at an undergraduate level, encompasses a wide range of genres, and comes with a compact disc with twenty-seven musical selections.

An Introduction to America's Music, Richard Crawford: Crawford's textbook takes a catholic approach to American music that gives vernacular music and folk genres appropriate attention.

Invisible Empire: Bob Dylan's Basement Tapes, Greil Marcus: This very personal and revisionist book looks back at the music of Dylan but, equally important, at various other individuals, such as Dock Boggs, who helped shape twentieth-century folk and folk-based music.

Jimmie Rodgers: The Life & Times of America's Blue Yodler, Nolan Porterfield: Porterfield has written the definitive study of Rodger's brief and influential life.

Klezmer: Jewish Music from Old World to Our World, Henry Sapoznik: This is the best survey of this genre, which includes its history as well as the story of the author's own involvement in the revival of interest in this genre.

The Life and Legend of Lead Belly, Kip Lornell and Charles K. Wolfe: This is a carefully written biography of one of America's most highly regarded and influential black folk singers.

Long Steel Rail, 2nd ed., Norm Cohen: This classic study of its subject is encapsulated in its subtitle: "The Railroad in American Folk Song."

Louisiana Music: A Journey from R&B to Zydeco, Jazz to Country, Blues to Gospel, Cajun Music to Swamp Pop to Carnival Music and Beyond, Rick Koster: Enjoy this journalistic voyage through Louisiana's music as well as its related history, culture, and food.

Lydia Mendoza: Norteno, Tejano Legacies, Yolanda Broyles-Gonzalez: This is a bilingual edition of Broyles-Gonzalez's fine study detailing the life and significance of one of Latin music's most towering figures.

Making People's Music: Moe Asch and Folkways Records, Peter D. Goldsmith: This interesting biography of Folkways founder Moses

Asch includes the history of the label and its impact on American cultural history.

Milton Brown and the Founding of Western Swing, Cary Ginnell, with special assistance from Roy Lee Brown: This is the most comprehensive book on western swing yet, which focuses on the development of this important genre in Texas and Oklahoma during the early to middle 1930s.

Mountains of Music: West Virginia Traditional Music from Goldenseal, compiled by John Lilly: Lilly compiled twenty-three of the best pieces about Mountain State folk music that were first published in the state magazine *Goldenseal* from the 1970s through the 1990s.

Music Makers: Portraits and Songs from the Roots of America (with Audio CD), Tim Duffy: This lavishly illustrated (with photographs) book discusses the southern folk musicians who have been helped by the Music Maker Relief Foundation.

Musics of Multi-Cultural America, Kip Lornell and Anne Rasmussen: The riot grrrls are clearly pop, but most of the rest of the twelve musical communities described in these essays are folk or folk-based, including chapters on Native American and several Hispanic genres. The book is accompanied by a compact disc.

My Song Is My Weapon, Robbie Leiberman: This is a personal and heartfelt look at left-wing politics and folk music with a strong focus on the period between 1935 and 1970.

The New Grove Dictionary of American Music, edited by Wiley Hitchcock and Stanley Sadie: This four-volume reference set contains hundreds of well-written entries related to American folk music.

Only a Miner, Archie Green: Green takes a multi-faceted approach to this intriguing study of coal mining songs and culture.

Pistol Packin' Mama: Aunt Molly Jackson and the Politics of Folksong, Shelly Romalis: Romalis takes a close look not only at Jackson's fascinating life, but also how it fit into the political climates of the 1920s through the 1950s.

Polka Happiness, Charles Keil, Angeliki Keil, and Dick Blau: The essays written by this trio examine the musical culture of polka as well as the importance of this music in establishing ethnic identity.

Positively 4th Street: The Lives and Times of Joan Baez, Bob Dylan, Mimi Baez Farina, and Richard Farina, David Hajdu: Read this heartfelt look at the relationships among these four important figures in the folk revival that swept the United States in the late 1950s and early 1960s.

Puro Conjunto: An Album in Words and Pictures, edited by Juan Tejeda: This is a wide-ranging collection of writings (scholarly essays, articles by journalists and music critics, interviews with legendary performers, autobiographical accounts, short stories, and poetry) about various aspects of conjunto music. The graphics (photos and posters) add greatly to the impact of this book.

Rainbow Quest: The Folk Music Revival and American Society, 1940–1970, Ronald Cohen: Drawing on extensive interviews and personal experience, Cohen reconstructs the history of this singular cultural moment, tracing its origins to the early decades of the twentieth century and suggests its ramifications for music today.

Red River Blues: The Blues Tradition in the South, Bruce Bastin: This is the definitive study of the history and development of

African American folk blues in Georgia and the Carolinas.

River of Song, Theo Pelletier (photographer), John Funkerman, and Elijah Wald: A companion to the PBS-broadcast film and the multi-CD set issued by Smithsonian Folkways, this book examines vernacular, folk, and folk-based music found along the Mississippi River from Minnesota to Louisiana.

Romancing the Folk: Public Memory and American Roots Music, Benjamin Filene: Filene's case studies of the lives and careers of Muddy Waters, Willie Dixon, Pete Seeger, and others demonstrate how they intersected with culture brokers, middlemen, and record company employees who helped shape the perceptions of American folk music.

Singing the Glory Down, Lynwood Montell: This is a well-written study of non-professional family-oriented southern gospel groups in south central Kentucky.

Songsters & Saints: Vocal Traditions on Race Records, Paul Oliver: This is a masterful study of African American folk music heard on commercial recordings from the 1920s and 1930s.

The Sounds of People and Places—Readings in the Geography of American Folk and Popular Music, 3rd ed., edited by George O. Carney: This series of essays about the geographical implications of American folk and popular music in the twentieth century includes an extensive and helpful bibliography.

Sounds of the South, edited by Daniel W. Patterson: This volume of essays explores the richness of southern traditional music from shout singing in the South Carolina sea islands to Cajun fiddling to Mexican American conjunto music.

Southern Exposure: The Story of Southern Music in Pictures and Words, Richard Carlin: This book includes revealing photographs and evocative descriptions covering a wide range of folk and folk-based musical styles of the American South from the 1850s to World War II.

The Study of Folk Music in the Modern World, Philip Bohlman: This is written as a scholarly and thoughtful approach to the problems of defining folk music in our postmodern world.

Texas-Mexican Conjunto: History of a Working-Class Music, Manuel Pena: This is the best scholarly, yet fully accessible, book about conjunto, which remains very popular along the Texas-Mexican border.

Transforming Tradition: Folk Music Revivals Examined, edited by Neil V. Rosenberg: Some very personal and revealing essays about blues and old-time music, among others, are included in this insightful book.

The United States and Canada (Garland Encyclopedia of World Music, Volume 3), edited by Ellen Koskoff: This very ambitious volume encompasses a wide variety of vernacular music, including most of the folk and ethnic traditions, such as blues and bluegrass, found throughout the United States.

Wasn't That a Time!: Firsthand Accounts of the Folk Music Revival, edited by Ron Cohen: This useful (and sometimes provocative) set of essays takes a variety of perspectives on the history and significance of the 1950s and 1960s folk revival.

When We Were Good: The Folk Revival, Robert Cantwell: This scholarly, provocative, accessible examination of the folk revival and its roots goes as far back as minstrelsy.

"The Whorehouse Bells Were Ringing" and Other Songs Cowboys Sing, collected and edited by Guy Logsdon: Logsdon's greatly entertaining book about late-nineteenth- and twentieth-century cowboy songs is quite informative and includes some rather bawdy material.

Zydeco!, Ben Sandmal: This solidly written and entertaining trip through this music is greatly enhanced by Rick Olivier's wonderful black and white photographs.

Magazines

Most of these magazines are owned and edited by fans and not academic scholars. While they often focus on personalities and musical history, these magazines offer substantial amounts of information that is often unavailable elsewhere. Most of them can be found at magazine stands in major cities and all of them maintain their own Web site, the address for which can be found via your favorite search engine.

Bluegrass Unlimited: This grandmother of all magazines devoted to this music has been going strong for decades.

Dirty Linen: This magazine is devoted to "Folk and World Music" and contains many articles, reviews, and information about American music topics.

Folk Works: Billing itself as "a newspaper dedicated to promoting Folk Music, Dance, Storytelling, and other folk arts in the greater Los Angeles area" this publication can be found either in hard copy or online.

Living Blues: Now based at Old Miss (The University of Mississippi), this magazine remains the strongest and most interesting American-based journal to cover blues.

Mugwamps: Since 1971, editor Michael Holmes has provided a central place where people interested in folk music could "buy, sell, trade and learn about the musical instruments . . . and anything else . . . of interest to readers."

Musical Traditions: Like *Dirty Linen*, this fine U.K. magazine wanders throughout the world of music but quite often lands in the United States.

Old Time Herald: The successor (of sorts) to *Old Time Music*, this magazine covers "old time music" in all of its manifestations.

Sing Out!: Since the 1950s, *Sing Out!* has brought information about the folk music scene to eager readers throughout the world.

Web Sites

In this new millennium more and more traditional music can be found on the Web. There are sites for folk festivals and clubs, record companies, and non-profit organizations devoted to American folk music. In addition, the Web is home to various mailing lists, chat rooms, and sites for blues, old-time music, bluegrass, Cajun, klezmer, and so forth. In fact nearly all forms of American folk and grassroots music now enjoy a presence on the Internet. Here are some of the most significant ones, with their most recent addresses included. Some of these groups, organizations, or companies have been around for decades and should maintain their Web presence for the upcoming years. Their precise location can be reconfirmed by using the search engine of your choice.

American Folklore Society (www.afsnet.org): Founded in 1888, this scholarly society is not exclusively focused on music, but

American folk music is often included in its journal and panels at its annual meetings.

Arhoolie Records/Flower Films (www.arhoolie.com): Chris Strachwitz founded Arhoolie in 1960 to record Texas Songster Mance Lipscomb, and it has blossomed into one of the most important small record companies to explore American folk (and related) musical genres.

Festival Finder (www.festivalfinder.com/folk): This handy site helps locate music festivals of all kinds, including blues, bluegrass, folk, and other related genres.

Folk Alliance (www.folk.org): This is an umbrella for organizations that exist to foster and promote traditional, contemporary, and multicultural folk music and dance, and related performing arts in North America.

Folk Era Records (www.folkera.com): Since 1985 this company has issued nearly 100 records focusing on "the time period of folk music's greatest popularity, the decade between 1957 and 1967." Folk Era has an interesting array of new and reissued material by groups as diverse as The Brothers Four, The Chad Mitchell Trio, The Tarriers, and The Kingston Trio.

Folk Music Archives™—Voice Preservation of American Folk Music (http://folkmusicarchives.org): This site promotes itself as a site devoted to digital interviews of American folk artists, groups, and venues of the 1950s and 1960s.

Folklife Center of the Library of Congress (www.loc.gov/folklife): This agency was created by Congress in 1976 "to preserve and present American Folklife." The center incorporates the Archive of Folk Culture, which was established at the library in 1928 as a repository for American folk music. The center and its collections have grown to encompass all aspects of folklore and folklife from this country and around the world.

Roots and Rhythm (www.rootsandrhythm.com): Of all the Internet or mail-order record sites with comprehensive catalogs, this is perhaps the best.

Rounder Records (www.rounder.com): First conceived by three college students in 1970 as an antiprofit collective, Rounder has evolved into a large multifaceted company with scores of American folk music titles in its catalog.

Shanachie Entertainment (www.shanachie.com): This umbrella organization includes films, a fine record reissue series (Yazoo), and contemporary music releases, many of which touch on American folk music.

Singing News (www.singingnews.com): "The Printed Voice of Southern Gospel Music" has long been a print advocate for this important genre and it can now be accessed electronically.

Smithsonian Folkways (www.folkways.si.edu): Before his death, Moe Asch and the Smithsonian Institution reached a deal whereby the institution would keep Asch's Folkways back catalog in print as well as carry his mission forward with new releases.

Society for American Music (www.american-music.org): Founded in the mid-1970s, the Society for American Music consists mostly of academic folks with broad-ranging interests, including many folk and folk-based genres.

Society for Ethnomusicology (www.indiana.edu/~ethmusic): Since the 1950s, members of this society have examined, described, and taught courses about a wide-range of non-classical music, including American folk music.

Southern Gospel (www.sogospel.com): This Web site is devoted to the history and dissemination of southern gospel music.

Viewing

A strong documentary film with a comprehensive booklet not only provides you with important information but brings an immediacy to the music that can't be found on the printed page. Film allows you to hear and see a musical culture or musical performance. When it's done right, viewing a documentary film is the next best thing to being there.

Appalachian Journey (Vestapol Films, 1998): This video is an anthology of White-American folk music that includes performances by old-time banjo player and storyteller Frank Proffitt Jr. and bluegrass musician Raymond Fairchild.

Chase the Devil: Religious Music of the Appalachians (Shanchie Entertainment, 1990): This BBC documentary was filmed in the early 1980s mostly in southwestern Virginia. It features powerful holiness preaching and singing, a riverside baptism, and God's Little Elvis.

Dave Van Ronk in Concert (Shanachie Entertainment, 1991): This features informal interviews and concert footage from a concert at Ohio University circa 1980 by a man who was at the core of the folk revival in New York City.

Deep Blues (Robert Mugge Films, 1993): This engaging film takes its name from Robert Palmer's insightful book about the history and cultural significance of blues in the Mississippi River Delta.

Del Mero Corazon ("Straight from Their Heart"): Love Songs of the Southwest (Flower Films, 1979): The music, history, and culture of the lengthy and important Mexican-American border is the focus of this film.

Doc & Merle: The Lives and Music of Doc & Merle Watson (Vestapol Films, 1992): This documentary with performance footage covers these important western North Carolina guitarists.

Don't Look Back—Bob Dylan (New Video Group, 1967): D. A. Pennebaker's black-and-white revealing documentary focuses on Dylan's controversial 1965 tour.

Dreams and Songs of the Noble (Vestapol Films, 1991): As part of the Alan Lomax Collection, this anthology includes interviews and brief performances by half a dozen of America's best folk singers, such as blues man Sam Chatmon, fiddler Tommy Jarrell, and balladeer Nimrod Workman.

Folk City 25th Anniversary Concert (Rhino, 1987): Arlo Guthrie, Tom Paxton, and Joan Baez are among the participants in this pleasant performance/documentary about this famous New York City folk club.

High Lonesome: The Story of Bluegrass (Shanachie Entertainment, 1994): This film, which features interviews and performances by Bill Monroe, Jimmy Martin, The Osborne Brothers, and Alison Krauss, remains the best visual documentary about bluegrass.

Hot Pepper: The Life and Music of Clifton Chenier (Flower Films, 1973): Another fine Les Blank film, this one focuses on Clifton Chenier, the King of Zydeco.

In Heaven There Is No Beer (Flower Films, 1984): This is an entertaining ethnographic examination of Midwestern polka music and culture.

A Jumpin' Night in the Garden of Eden (First Run Features, 1987): This documentary incorporates contemporary performances with historical photographs to produce an overview of klezmer music from the 1920s through its revival in the 1980s.

Kumu Hula: Keepers of a Culture (Robert Mugge Films, 1989): Documentarian Mugge's film examines contemporary hula and its related musical culture in Hawaii.

Land Where the Blues Began (Vestapol, 1990): From Alan Lomax's American Patchwork film series, this one brings work songs, fife and drum bands, and diddley-bows into your living room.

Louie Bluie (Pacific Arts Home Video, 1986): The life and creative energies of Howard Armstrong, an African American fiddle playing genius, is the focus of Terry Zwigoff's film.

The Mississippi River of Song (Acorn Media Publishing, 1999): This lengthy journey about the musical culture along the Mississippi River from New Orleans northward to Minnesota was originally aired on PBS in early 1999. The four one-hour programs are now available separately for home viewing.

A Musical Journey: The Films of Pete, Toshi & Dan Seeger, 1957–1961 (Vestapol Films 1996): This low-tech but compelling video consists of home movies of Big Bill Broonzy, The McPeake Family, Pete Steele, and others filmed by Pete Seeger, his spouse, and son.

Sacred Steel (Arhoolie Foundation Films, 2001): The work of several contemporary African American steel guitarists living and performing in Holiness churches between Florida and New York City are documented in this entertaining film.

Say Amen, Somebody (Xenon Studios, 1980): The Reverend Thomas A. Dorsey and Willie Mae Ford Smith are among the two important artists featured in this moving documentary about African American gospel music.

Spend It All (Flower Films, 1971): Les Blank's evocative film focuses on Cajun culture and music.

Sprout Wings and Fly (Flower Films, 1983): An interesting, entertaining, and insightful documentary examining the life and musical culture of the North Carolina fiddling legend Tommy Jarrell.

Take Me Back to Tulsa: An Anthology of Western Swing (Vestapol Films, 2000): This is a compilation of short, vintage clips of western swing by such important artists as Bob Wills, Tommy Duncan, and Hank Thompson.

Traditional Music Classics: Featuring Doc Watson, Roscoe Holcomb, Buell Kazee & Kilby Snow (Shanachie Entertainment, 1997): Informal footage of 1960s and 1970s performances by these important old-time Appalachian artists constitute this engaging film.

Troubadours of Folk: The Greatest Gathering of Folk Musicians in 25 Years (Rhino, 1993): These selections come from a large 1993 concert that includes performances by Arlo Guthrie, Ritchie Havens, and Joni Mitchell.

Index

About the Author

Kip Lornell has been researching and writing about American roots music since the late 1960s. Since 1973, he has lived and worked in the South, mostly on music-related films, record projects, and books. Currently teaching in the Music Department at the George Washington University, he is the author of eight books, including *The Life and Legend of Lead Belly* (with Charles Wolfe), *Introducing American Folk Music: Grassroots and Ethnic Traditions in the United States*, and *Happy in the Service of the Lord: African American Gospel Quartets in Memphis*. He was awarded the 1992 ASCAP-DEEMS Taylor Award for the best book about American music and a 1997 Grammy Award for his writing, which appeared in the booklet accompanying the Anthology of American Folk Music issued by Smithsonian Folkways.